PARENTING WHEN YOU'RE AUTISTIC

Tips and advice on how to parent successfully alongside your neurodivergence

Pooky Knightsmith

Foreword by Nerys Hughes

Jessica Kingsley Publishers
London and Philadelphia

First published in Great Britain in 2025 by Jessica Kingsley Publishers
An imprint of John Murray Press

2

A CIP catalogue record for this title is available from the British Library and the Library of Congress

ISBN 978 1 83997 878 4
eISBN 978 1 83997 879 1

Printed and bound in Great Britain by Bell & Bain Limited

Jessica Kingsley Publishers' policy is to use papers that are natural, renewable and recyclable products and made from wood grown in sustainable forests. The logging and manufacturing processes are expected to conform to the environmental regulations of the country of origin.

Jessica Kingsley Publishers
Carmelite House
50 Victoria Embankment
London EC4Y 0DZ

www.jkp.com

John Murray Press
Part of Hodder & Stoughton Ltd
An Hachette Company

For Ellie and Nerys,
who inspire me to learn more,
love more and laugh more.

Contents

Foreword

I am so grateful to Pooky for writing the book so many parents need to read. When Pooky came into my life it was during the Covid-19 pandemic. In her wonderful autistic way she asked me to help other parents by making a list of things parents could do to manage. I, being my ADHD self, exclaimed, 'A list? NEVER?' Sorry, nothing so concrete from me. My answer in short was, 'There are not enough hours in our day; the task at hand is not viable; what we all need is to drink wine and admit we are not going to get all of this done!' And so a friendship was formed. I am the honest, Puck-like, disruptor; Pooky, the goddess of structure and curator of order. Together we travel the country. Pooky with her neatly ordered, well-thought-through mnemonics, me with my scattered hypotheses, rapid pace, gut-wrenching honesty, doing things that make Pooky shudder like changing my workshop five minutes before we go on stage. In truth we should be each other's trigger warning, but we are not, because as we find in this book, we saw each other: our neuroradar was strong. We found a safe place in the sea of normative expectations. Full confession: we do have our human shield, the ever neurotypical, well-regulated and deeply compassionate agent Ellie, our work mother, who makes sure we get from A to B and remember to eat.

What we have had from the very first day is a sense of acceptance, knowing, joy, a place to ask, 'What do you think?' 'Is this okay?' Or 'Guess what my amazing child did today?' During our journey, we have taken our own children through a number of obstacles, suspensions, school non-attendance, provisions, bullying, home schooling, and the worst of the worst: our children stating they hate themselves, they feel not good enough, they are not safe. We shared fears, tears, hurt, frustration and of course solutions. When Pooky tentatively told me of the book's content and her approach of asking our community for their voice, I was overjoyed. I have spent my career forging a safe place for children and their families, and have been witness to so many dehumanizing approaches thrust on both parents and children in the name of normalizing us all. So many times being spoken at, spoken for, when really, here, within our community, the answers exist.

I have worked with heroic parents and children. It has been a privilege and an honour to be part of so many lives, to see so much beauty, courage and magic. For so much of my career I was the salmon swimming up the river in the opposite direction to all the other fish. In the last decade, I have found other fish, swimming my way. A community has formed, voices have come together and a chorus of voices have found some harmony. Of course, it's not enough. We still have a waiting list, our doors are still open, because the world still needs shaping and colouring to include our glorious spectrum. It was time our community was given space to accept and find our own still-fragile, worthwhile voice over the noise of conforming, normalizing and of course masking. This book gives us all a space to breathe, to make a list (if you like to). Warning. You may laugh, you will likely cry, but you will find something that resonates. Pooky, with the shared voice of our community, reminds us that we can bond and connect. We should and can find joy and acceptance. We do need to care for ourselves as much as, if not more than, we do our children.

Nerys Hughes
Neurodivergent parent
Founder of Whole Child Therapy
www.wholechildtherapy.com
@wct_team

Acknowledgements

My heartfelt thanks goes to those who shared their ideas and experiences. Some of them are named here, some chose to remain anonymous:

Alexander, Ali B, Alice Boon, Alice Hoyle, Alison, Amanda Patterson, Amelia, Amy Montiel, Andrea, Andy, Anna Putt, Annette Rinner, Ayesha Pusey, Bea, Becky Munn, Carol Fare, Carter, Catherine, Cathryn, Cathy Williams, Cheryl Stafford, Chrissa Wadlow, Claire Garrett, Claire Harmsworth, Daisy Owen, Daniel, Dave Straughan, David Marsden, Deb Faulkner, Di, Donna Thomas, Dylan Jones, Eleanor Hase, Ellice, Ellie, Emma D., Emma Hollis, Emma Whittaker, Fran Lewis, G.M., Helen Edgar, Helen MacIntosh, Ian Horsewell, James Koppert, Jo, Joe, Jo Jeffries, Jonas Vils, Julie Price, Jus, Kaitlynn Bailey-Park, Karen, Kat Cannon, Kate Carré, Katie Manson, Kerry Ann Gallagher, Kirsty, Lorna McCollum, Lou Fraser, Lucy Poole, Maddie K., Maria, Marie Featherstone, Mark, Mary Potsig, Mel Wiltshire, Naomi Hockley, Pamela Melling, Paul Rosser, Perinne Harding, Rachael Littlewood, Rachel Nurse, Rachel S., Raph, Rebecca Wozencroft, Robert Ward, Rosie, Ruth, Sam Holmes, Samuel, Sara, Sarah Evans, Sarah Jane Clark, Sarah-Jane Critchley, Si, Sian McDonald, Simon B., Sophia, Sophie, Stef, Stefan, Steph, Susi Jacobs, Tricia Elliott, Verity, Victoria Machin, Vince W.

My thanks too to Amy Lankester-Owen at Jessica Kingsley Publishers who wrote the proposal for this book and got it greenlit after I shared a very loose idea with her in the hope that she might think it was a good one. Her suggestions and guidance also proved invaluable in helping a butterfly of a book emerge from a rather ugly caterpillar of a first draft. The Big Edit happened whilst I was on a paragliding trip in the French Alps; my deepest thanks go to Rich and Marianne whose friendship and flexibility enabled me to (mostly) manage on the ground and in the air.

And finally, thanks to my elderly cat and constant writing companion Mork. This book would have been finished rather more quickly without your input, but the process would have been a lot less joyful.

Introduction

Welcome to this book, which aims to provide guidance, support and empowerment to neurodivergent parents on their parenting journey. Neurodivergent individuals are those whose neurological functioning differs from the neurotypical population, encompassing conditions such as autism, attention-deficit hyperactivity disorder (ADHD) and other brain-related variances.

This is the book I wish I could have read a little earlier on my parenting journey. I'm a late-diagnosed autistic mother of two autistic daughters (one biological, one adopted). Parenting has been the greatest privilege in the world, but it's certainly not been easy.

Casting around desperately for advice on how on earth to live well and parent well as an autistic adult, I found myself drawing blanks, so I decided to do the research and write the book that so many of us desperately need. I've had over a hundred neurodivergent adults share their experiences and ideas to shape the content; you'll see their voices woven throughout the book – in addition to the illustrative quotes, most of the ideas in the 'quick read' sections are direct quotes from the community. I'm excited by what we've created together because it has the potential to bring profound change to many neurodivergent parents and carers out there. The process of researching and writing it has transformed my own outlook and actions, and many of those who've contributed have remarked on how the conversations we've had and the ideas we've shared have helped their parenting to blossom.

This book is for anyone who wants to read it. Maybe you've done waiting lists and diagnostics, and had a bunch of reports to 'prove' your neurodivergence. Maybe you self-identify as autistic or ADHD, or maybe you're still at the wondering stage, just curious or reading with a partner or significant other in mind. Whatever. You're welcome here.

You're also welcome here no matter what shape your family takes. In my home we have two children, my husband, myself, my mother-in-law and a whole bunch of pets; but maybe you're a lone parent, a gay parent, a foster carer, an uncle, or you're someone working hard to co-parent following separation. Whatever shape your family takes, this book is for you.

There is no right or wrong reader and I hope that whatever your neurotype and whatever the shape of your family, you'll feel welcomed and inspired by what you read.

Whilst you can use this book in any order you wish, I've provided a brief summary below of the order in which I've tackled things and what I was hoping to achieve in each section. The book will work well read cover to cover but, equally, you might choose to dive straight into any topic that appeals to you, or that feels pertinent right now. There are no rules.

There's a real mix of short punchy 'quick read' sections and longer 'in-depth' chapters to try and keep things interesting for my ADHD friends, whilst I hope that the logical structures that you'll see repeated throughout will appeal to my autistic friends.

Throughout the book, you'll find sections called 'Your Turn' that invite you to reflect and write down your thoughts. These sections are designed to help you personalize the information in the book to your own experiences and needs. You don't have to fill them in if you prefer not to, and you can always come back to them later. If you find that you have more to say than the space provided, feel free to use a journal or extra paper to continue your reflections.

Section 1: Cultivating Your Neurodivergent Potential

In this section, we embark on a journey of self-discovery and wellbeing. We explore topics like self-identity, self-care, and how to harness your unique neurodivergent strengths to foster positive relationships and build essential support networks.

Section 2: Navigating Neurodiversity's Challenges
Here, we delve into the challenges that neurodivergent parents often face. From sensory differences and handling unsupportive people to managing intense emotions like anger and anxiety, this section equips you with strategies to navigate these external and internal hurdles.

Section 3: Mastering Neurodivergent Parenting
This section guides you through the practical aspects of parenting whilst embracing your neurodivergent identity. We explore how to manage conflicts, handle social events and address various family dynamics.

Section 4: Finding Joy
Our final section is dedicated to helping you find joy in your parenting. We'll explore the pleasure to be found in embracing our authentic selves, hunt for the everyday joys that parenting can bring and consider how to celebrate the positives whilst reframing the negatives. The book ends with heart-warming stories from fellow parents, all echoing the resounding theme of joy in the beautiful chaos of neurodivergent family life.

I hope you'll find that this book is not just a guide but a companion on your neurodivergent parenting adventure. Throughout, I encourage you to reflect, connect with the content, and tailor it to your unique experiences. Your journey is personal, but hopefully the many voices shared in these pages will help you to feel a little less alone in it.

Love, Pooky x
@pookyh

Section 1

CULTIVATING YOUR NEURODIVERGENT POTENTIAL

In this section, we embark on a journey of self-discovery and wellbeing. We explore topics like self-identity, self-care and how to harness your unique neurodivergent strengths to foster positive relationships and build essential support networks.

CHAPTER 1

Quick Read: Self-Care

We cannot be the adults that our children need unless we first take care of ourselves. Children need good role models and adults who have the mental and physical bandwidth to meet their needs. So, we're going to consider self-care here, right at the start of the book, because it underpins all that is to follow.

Self-care was a topic that split the community during my research. Some people were quick to extol the virtues of self-care and talked about its absolute necessity in their day-to-day life. Others saw it as yet another social construct designed around the needs of neurotypicals and which didn't help them at all.

> **'What's the point? Why should we force what doesn't come naturally? People say you will feel better. Well, I don't. I just have to play catch-up to make up for the lost time.'**

> **'Lying around wasting my day with cucumber slices on my eyes is a hugely inefficient waste of my time and forced self-soothing will never trick me into believing my circumstances are anything other than the truth.'**

So, I share these top tips with a little trepidation and with the proviso that, as with all of the ideas in this book, it's about finding what resonates with you. Look for what feels like it could work in your life and perhaps make things feel more manageable. I loved this definition of self-care that came from a member of the community:

> **'Self-care is consciously looking after your own physical, medical, emotional needs and wellbeing. I think it can be a conscious, practical effort because you know it's needed, but it can also be a deeper, kinder care as well; one you'd apply to someone you love.'**

Self-care doesn't have to mean bubble baths and yoga, though it can be those things if they work for you. Self-care might mean rigid routines, gaming or reading books about meteorology.

Self-care is something that I personally neglected in the past. I put others first, in my work and in my home. I denied myself sleep, nutrition, compassion and fun. After a long period of breakdown and burnout in my thirties, I rebuilt my life and these days, self-care is a big component. For me, it looks like getting enough sleep, building in intense exercise like bouldering or hill-hiking, taking care to eat enough and making space for family, friends and fun. I used to think I didn't have time for self-care. It felt frivolous and time-wasting, but a few years into my self-care experiment, I can conclude that when I look after myself I'm able to be a better parent, partner and professional with less illness and more joy, so I intend to continue. Additionally, I'd be far happier for my children to copy my current behaviours than my past ones; I'm a much better self-care role model for them these days.

There is no right way to do self-care, but hopefully some of the tips below that were shared by the community might help you think about how to be a little kinder to yourself and look to carve out a little time and energy to care for yourself as well as for others.

- **Look forwards, not back:** Self-care isn't another stick to beat yourself with about not having 'got things right' in the past. It's learning what you need and how you can implement that going forward. How to incorporate it into your life, only you can answer. I am like an oil tanker: it takes me a long time to turn around, but the small changes have made a big difference to my course.
- **The whole family will benefit from your self-care:** Meeting your self-care needs in a timely way will benefit everyone in the long run. There is a way you can get what you need and live a balanced, more content life where you feel emotionally stable. It might mean some adjustments to your own and everyone else's expectations, but it is possible.

- **Do it every day:** Self-care is like brushing your teeth. You might not always feel like doing it, but it is an important and necessary part of every day. You have to put the effort in and make sure it happens. It keeps you healthy.
- **Share ideas amongst the family:** We talk often about making sure that every day we do something we love, get some fresh air and do some movement. We talk about what we've chosen that day. It is different for each of us. We also keep a notebook on the landing and most evenings before bed, write down something we've loved today. I love planting that seed of a great moment just before sleep.
- **You deserve it:** no matter how busy you are. It's like people say, put on your own oxygen mask before helping others. You can only do what you can do and sometimes it's okay just to do nothing if that's the self-care that works for you.
- **Self-care doesn't have to be some big event:** It shouldn't be yet another thing you are failing at. Have a cup of tea, listen to the birds, breathe, put on your favourite song. Wash your hair. Get your nails done.
- **Diarize it:** I put it in my schedule, so I have time set aside to do it, even if I'm feeling quite good. I tend to do self-care when the kids are in bed or at school.
- **Self-care to prevent rather than cure:** It helps me greatly to do maintenance self-care, rather than reacting to feeling depleted.
- **Work out how to motivate yourself:** I try to drink plenty of water each day. As I don't often feel thirsty it's a very conscious decision; I therefore bought myself some nice bottles that I liked, knowing it would motivate me to use them.
- **Don't be afraid to buck the norm:** Co-sleep with your child if that is what they need, give up the battle to force them to be alone and scared at night. Change the sleeping arrangements in your home so you do not spend hours on

the bedroom floor of your child's room, or sat on the landing outside their door. Just buy a big enough bed that you all fit in comfortably and ignore advice from well-meaning but autism-ignorant super-nannies.

- **Explain your needs to your children:** Explaining, even for young children, the needs you have as a parent and why can really help. My partner needs a lot of recovery time and cannot cope with things being out of place or noise. Trying to explain this to the children does help. It is hard but as always, keeping the dialogue open and honest helps. It's important to try and set boundaries. Our children know that our bedroom is out of bounds for them.
- **Think about your own personal scaffolding:** Who do you know who can love you and hold you up? One or two people who get you and make you feel stronger is enough.
- **Find activities that recharge your batteries:** Look for things that offer you a break from your thinking brain. Things that give you that sense of connecting with your body and going with the flow. Like painting, meditating, listening to a talking book whilst in a hammock, or something more energetic if that's what you need.
- **Seek awe and wonder:** Perhaps in the night sky, through time in nature or by appreciating art or music.
- **Get moving:** What can you do to move your body? Dancing, walking, somatic shaking...? It's so important for moving feelings and stress through and out of your body.
- **Wear what feels good:** I am learning how to physically be comfortable each day. I am reassessing my wardrobe and asking if I like wearing things or if I just think it's something I should wear (for fashion reasons or what I think work expects). I am also considering underwear and noticing how distracted my bras can make me with uncomfortable textures and pressures. I have realized how important it is to

be comfortable at a basic clothing level in order to not put unnecessary stress on myself throughout the day.

- **Be kind to your future self by planning ahead:** I become overwhelmed by cooking and all the processes around it – deciding what to eat, making a shopping list, buying everything, unpacking, then cooking every day. However, by making a weekly meal plan and doing my weekly shop I have taken away the daily task of having to decide what's for dinner and I avoid needing to go to the shops after work (or after school with my autistic son, which is a disaster). I am mentally exhausted after work so my previous decision-making means less processing at a time when I'm fighting off a shutdown.

SUGGESTED SELF-CARE ACTIVITIES

When I asked the community what works for them in terms of self-care activities, the answers were very varied; here is a selection. Perhaps some of these might work for you too or might inspire you to think up ideas of your own.

- Reducing demands and sensory overwhelm
- Writing lists
- Walking the dog
- Walking in the countryside
- Going for a run
- Breathing or mindfulness
- Talking things through
- Going to my room and lying on the bed: reading or just staring into space
- Taking time alone
- Sleeping in the spare room
- Sleeping under a weighted blanket
- Managing expectations of myself
- Being realistic and kind to myself
- Doing things that feed my creativity
- Taking a silent bath

- Looking at my food and fluid intake
- Dipping into my sensory box full of calming things
- Snuggling in a heated blanket
- Diffusing my favourite scented oils to either calm or energize
- Eating favourite foods
- Locking myself in a room and not coming out for a bit
- Getting creative in a quiet space
- Organizing, tidying and ordering things
- Watching trashy TV
- Taking a night away with my partner
- Taking time off work
- Taking quiet time alone, reading, baking, gardening, drawing, tidying, almost anything as long as it's done in a relaxed way, not a whirlwind of urgency
- Eating alone
- Stepping into nature and stopping to take notice of the sights and sounds
- People-watching
- Journaling
- Reading in a nook or hammock
- Crocheting or knitting
- Heavy exercise: running, lifting, climbing
- Something fun and active that fills your whole mind, like ice hockey
- Singing in a choir
- Revisiting happy memories through photographs
- Facetiming a friend who gets it
- Watching my favourite show
- Anything that makes me laugh
- Writing either with or without purpose, depending on my mood
- Watching my lava lamp
- Stroking a pet
- Weeding or watering my garden

In this chapter, we've explored the diverse perspectives on self-care within our community. For some, self-care is an essential practice, whilst for others, it may not come naturally. Regardless of where you stand, it's essential to remember that self-care isn't a one-size-fits-all concept. It's about finding what resonates with you, what makes your daily life more manageable, and what allows you to care for yourself as you care for others. Whether it's a simple cup of tea, a walk in nature, or planning ahead to ease life's demands, self-care is an act of kindness towards yourself.

YOUR TURN

As you engage with the 'Your Turn' reflection activities, consider how you can integrate self-care into your daily routine, benefiting not only yourself but also your family's wellbeing.

Reflect on your current understanding of self-care. Has it been a concept you've embraced or struggled with? Share any personal experiences related to self-care that have shaped your perspective.

....

....

....

....

Consider the analogy that self-care is like brushing your teeth – a daily necessity. How can you integrate self-care into your daily routine? Are there specific self-care activities that resonate with you?

....

....

....

....

Share your thoughts on the idea that self-care can benefit not only you but also your family. How do you envision implementing self-care practices that contribute to a more balanced and content family life?

....

....

....

....

Think about the self-care strategies mentioned by the community in the 'Suggested Self-Care Activities' box above. Are there any activities that particularly stand out for you? How might you incorporate them into your self-care routine?

....

....

....

....

Reflect on the concept of self-care as a form of kindness to your future self. Have you already implemented any strategies, like planning ahead or creating routines to ease daily stressors? If not, how might you start incorporating these practices into your life?

....

....

....

....

CHAPTER 2

In-Depth: Developing Positive Parent–Child Relationships

It can be challenging to develop a positive relationship with our children when just managing ourselves day to day can feel like a pretty tall order. My research showed, though, that there are lots of things we can do to support the development of relationships that work for our unique families. I was also excited to discover that as well as some pretty hefty challenges, there were also some aspects of our relationships that were enhanced compared to those experienced by our neurotypical peers.

An important thing to remember whilst reading this chapter is there is no right way and wrong way, only the way that works for you and your family. It's also important to remember that you're not alone in any struggles you're facing, so please try not to beat yourself up too much. Finally, things can change. I remember being terrified at the prospect of becoming a mum. I didn't think I had it in me to develop a meaningful relationship with a child and I was quite sure I didn't have the requisite levels of patience and compassion needed. It didn't come naturally to me; mine was not an instant perfect love, but one that grew over time. It's still growing and I'm always trying to learn more and work on it. My daughters are teenagers now and I love them more than I ever have, though there are days when I question **everything**. They have taught me a lot about love and relationships and as they get older, and I gain in confidence, we're able to genuinely enjoy each other more and more.

Before diving into ideas to support you in your relationships, I'm going to share the experiences of other neurodivergent parents and carers. I'm going to share the challenges first before sharing the good bits of their relationships. This is to help you realize you're not alone in this journey if you're struggling. But there is reason to be hopeful; we are absolutely able to develop brilliant relationships with our children. Sure, things might look a bit different in our homes than in other people's, but that doesn't have to be a bad thing.

Shared Experiences: The Lows

When I asked parents and carers to share challenges they faced in their relationships with their children, this is what they said:

> **'We are poles apart and rarely see eye to eye.'**
>
> **'She often doesn't feel my love, respect, humour, compassion or empathy, as I do these things in a way that she can't access.'**
>
> **'They think I am being lazy when I am overwhelmed. They think I'm being attention-seeking when I'm being creative.'**
>
> **'My child is exuberant, noisy and constantly moving and climbing. It often feels too overwhelming and I am often unable to find a quiet place to regulate myself.'**
>
> **'I get so tired and depleted. My children are demanding and draining. I want to meet their needs in a superhuman way because they are wonderful human beings, but their self-confidence and self-belief is very low due to the world breaking their hearts too many times.'**
>
> **'It's hard when their needs impact on mine, for instance I need some time and space to myself to regulate and they need me to co-regulate; or my son needs music and movement to help him and I need peace and calm.'**
>
> **'I haven't been very honest with my children about my own childhood. They have mostly been very secure and have strong attachments, but I did not experience that growing up. I have been determined not to let my dysfunctional family impact on my own children but I am not sure that this has helped them to understand me.'**

'I didn't have patience with him when he was a toddler playing with toys. I couldn't see the point of some games.'

'When her anxiety is building, I find mine rises too because I want to take it away from her but I can't, and this leads to me feeling helpless and sad.'

'My youngest is chaos incarnate. He makes mess, he does not mind food on his hands and face, and he goes from one task to another very quickly. This can be very triggering for me, especially food mess. I try to remind myself this is normal development for a one-year-old but I can't help but feel like he is doing it on purpose.'

'I like to run to timescales to prevent anxiety. My children don't like to have the same routines, structures or timescales as my own. This causes anxiety and frustration.'

'I'm often trying really hard to control my own anxiety or emotions when trying to listen or be present with them. I'm always on the go or doing things whilst listening. I worry that they don't feel heard or understood and that I don't model focus and calm.'

Shared Experiences: The Highs

When I asked parents and carers to share the best bits about their relationships with their children, this is what they said:

'They trust me to believe what they tell me about their experience or feelings and they are absolutely certain that I love them.'

'They are forgiving of my frequent mistakes and compassionate for my flaws whilst still declaring me the best mamma in the world.'

'Being an autistic mother to two autistic children, I am better able to empathize with their experiences. I can also share in their sensory joy.'

'I like not following the rules. I like to follow what works well for us. It is often not what everyone else is doing.'

'We have a very open and honest relationship. They know my triggers and I know theirs.'

'My neurodiverse son and I have a true connection I cannot put into words. I am able to advocate for him in ways no one else can because no one else understands what he is going through as much as me, his neurodiverse mother. We do not need words.'

'We have oodles of empathy and an enormous amount of consideration for one another.'

'We respect downtime and celebrate mistakes and learning. There is just so much love!'

'We have a very open and honest relationship. He will tell me about everything including maybe things I would rather not know about!'

10 THINGS YOU NEED TO HEAR

Here are ten things that I and other autistic parents/carers thought it was important for you to hear:

1. It's normal not to always enjoy parenthood.
2. It's okay to politely ignore the suggestions and advice of others.
3. Don't try to be a neurotypical parent. It won't work.
4. You are not a bad parent, you are a different parent.
5. It's okay to get stuff wrong. Apologize to your kids when this happens.

6. You have your limits – this is okay to admit and not okay to ignore.
7. Try not to feel guilty about not being able to do it all.
8. It is up to you and your child to decide how your relationship looks.
9. You are good enough. You are not perfect, but that's okay.
10. You cannot be kind to your children unless you are kind to yourself.

The Ideas

For each theme in this book, we explore a range of ideas that you can adapt for use in your day-to-day life. These ideas are all inspired by fellow neurodivergent parents and carers who've shared what works for them. Take a look and cherry-pick the ideas that you think might work for you right now. You can always revisit the others later.

The ideas explored in the following pages are:

- **Idea 1: Embrace Being a Successful Neurodivergent Parent, Not a Failed Neurotypical One**
- **Idea 2: Bond Quietly**
- **Idea 3: Clear Expectations**
- **Idea 4: Enjoy the Child You Have**
- **Idea 5: Be Open and Honest**
- **Idea 6: Have One-to-One Time**
- **Idea 7: Take Time for You**
- **Idea 8: Listen**
- **Idea 9: Lean into Fun**
- **Idea 10: Forgive the Ruptures and Focus on Repair**

Idea 1: Embrace Being a Successful Neurodivergent Parent, Not a Failed Neurotypical One

It can be easy to compare ourselves to other parents and find that we're not matching up. There are a myriad reasons for this, not least that we're often comparing our bloopers reel with the highlights reel that everyone else chooses to share whilst their bloopers are left on the cutting room floor. Even so, as neurodivergent parents we will have different strengths and challenges than our neurotypical peers and we are likely to parent a little differently in consequence. And that's okay. The very best way to parent is the way that works well for you and your family, regardless of what is 'typical' or 'normal'.

Forgiving yourself for doing things the way that works for you and viewing this through the lens of success as a neurodivergent parent rather than failure at attempting a neurotypical route is one way to relieve a lot of the burden of feeling not good enough every day.

You are good enough, you just do things a little differently and that's okay. In fact, it's more than okay because sometimes the way you do things will be better than the norm.

Five Things You Could Try

1. **Ask friends and family about your parenting strengths:** Even if you feel like you're getting it wrong a lot of the time, the chances are that those who live with and love you would be able to tell you about all the things you do get right. We can become quite blind to these in our day-to-day life so actually asking our family or friends can be eye-opening. Whilst it might feel a little bit awkward to ask someone to list out our strengths, it can be both affirming and surprising to hear what they have to say.

   Many of the parents who contributed to this book did this exercise and wrote me emails of thanks for prompting them to do so as it felt so good. Many of them discovered that some of the things they considered weaknesses were in fact seen as strengths by their children. You can also return the favour and tell a friend or family member about the things that make them a great parent in your eyes. Our neurotypical peers often have a lot of parenting hang-ups too. They may take a different shape than ours but years of working with parents and carers has taught me that many of the really good ones feel like they're not doing a good enough job.

2. **Cleanse your social media feeds:** One of the things that can really contribute to the constant feeling of 'not good enough' and comparing our parenting with that of others is our social media feeds. Being regularly confronted with the highlights of other people's parenting journey when we are just about managing to make it through each day can feel like being constantly beaten down. Take a good look at the accounts you follow and ask yourself honestly whether they are net positive or net negative when it comes to your mood and feelings about yourself.

   Cleansing our feed and removing the accounts that most often make our stomachs twist can make a big difference. You might choose to replace them with people who feel more like your tribe, people who get it and perhaps face similar challenges to yourself or who are simply more honest and authentic in their journey. This exercise might cause you to stop and reflect on who you spend time with in real life as well: if you find that the feeds you most want to delete due to their toxicity are those of people you regularly spend time with, then you might want to quietly consider whether the time you spend with those people is net positive or not. Some people are far more open and honest when you see them face to face, in which case fine. But, just as you don't have to continue to follow someone on social media if they make you feel terrible, you also do have some agency over who you would most like to spend time with face to face as well.

IDEAS OF PEOPLE TO FOLLOW ONLINE

If you'd like to leverage your social media channels for good and fill it with voices that might inspire you on your parenting journey as a neurodivergent adult, these are some voices that were recommended by the community:

Jodie Clarke (previously Smitten)

> **'Jodie is amazing because she totally gets the experience of being autistic and parenting autistic children. She is highly knowledgeable and has loads of resources on her website/ social media pages. If you're lucky, you can work with her directly. She really cares.'**

- Website: www.jodieclarke.co.uk
- Facebook: JodieClarkeWiltshire
- X (formerly Twitter): @JodieSmitten

Autistic Parents UK

Autistic Parents UK is an autistic-led charity committed to supporting autistic parents in a number of ways, including online peer support groups and monthly webinars.

- Website: www.autisticparentsuk.org/about
- Facebook: autisticparentsUK
- Instagram: @autistic_parents_uk
- X: @parentsautistic

Dean Beadle

Honest, deeply funny and doing brilliant work. A killer singer/ songwriter to boot!

- Website: deanbeadle.wordpress.com
- Facebook: dean.beadlespeaker
- X: @DeanBeadleUK

Heidi Mavir

Great on a no-holds barred and suitably sweary approach to life.

- Website: www.heidimavir.com
- Facebook: seNDSupport
- YouTube: www.youtube.com/@heidiwaddington
- X: @heidimavir

Kieran Rose

Author, consultant, speaker, trainer, autistic parent, situationally mute, rogue researcher specializing in autistic masking, stigma and identity.

- Website: theautisticadvocate.com
- YouTube: www.youtube.com/@TheAutisticAdvocate
- X: @ KieranRose7

Sarah-Jane Critchley

Supporting neurodivergent people and their loved ones and allies in achieving a joyful and fulfilling life.

- Website: www.differentjoy.com
- Instagram: @sarahjanecritchley
- X: @SarahJaneCritch

Pooky Knightsmith

Many of the community kindly recommended following me.

- Website: pookyknightsmith.com
- Instagram: @pookyh
- YouTube: youtube.com/pookyh
- Patreon: patreon.com/pookyh
- X: @pookyh

3. **Do more of what you do differently:** Everybody parents a little bit differently and that's okay. Instead of feeling ashamed of the parenting quirks that set you apart from the crowd, lean

into them. You'll have developed your parenting this way for a reason, and if there are approaches that work for you and feel manageable and good, do more of that, regardless of what everybody else seems to be doing.

4. **Have a go-to coping statement:** Coping statements can be a great way to displace difficult thoughts that circle in our heads. We can sometimes be our own worst enemies as our negative internal narrative is like a bully constantly lurking in the shadows waiting to pounce. Coping statements are phrases we decide upon which present a different viewpoint and which we can repeat again and again in an attempt to diffuse and displace the mean words of our inner bully.

   For example, if you often find yourself thinking, 'Why can't I do this? I'm useless,' you might counter this with a coping phrase such as 'I'm not useless, I'm autistic,' Or 'I can do this, but I need to be kind to myself first.'

CREATING COPING STATEMENTS

Thinking, at a time of calm, about the words we most need to hear from those we love can help us identify the best coping statements. Those statements might feel wrong in our mouths at first but with practice, they can become more helpful and you might even start to believe them.

Here are some coping statements suggested by fellow neurodivergent parents:

- I'm doing better than I think.
- Today is a hard day, it's okay to take it slowly.
- My children know they are loved, that is all that really matters.
- My way is okay.
- I am a good enough parent.
- I have done this before, I can do it again.
- I choose not to engage with these negative thoughts.

- I will do what I can and forgive myself for what I can't.
- I am a successful neurodivergent parent, not a failed neurotypical one.
- My children are fantastic, I am doing something right!

You may find that coming up with your own is a little harder but even more effective than borrowing someone else's.

5. **Delegate what you don't do well:** If there are other people with whom you are able to share some of the parenting load, it can be helpful to discuss the parts of parenting you find especially challenging. Some tasks that push you to breaking point may feel easier for a partner or parent who might be happy to relieve you of those tasks specifically. Delegating the tasks that you find most physically or emotionally exhausting can mean you are more able to engage with other parenting tasks.

   If you have a neurotypical partner or fellow parent, it's quite possible that you'll find that the bits of parenting that come more easily to you are the bits that they find most challenging and vice versa. This can make these conversations a win–win, with everyone doing more of what they enjoy and excel at whilst passing on those tasks they'd really rather not be doing.

Reflection

What's working well? What are you already doing? Could you do more of it?

....

....

....

....

What would you like to change?

What new ideas could you try?

My next tiny step is... What tiny step could you commit to taking today or tomorrow to work towards a different way of doing things?

Notes

Idea 2: Bond Quietly

Bonding can feel like a high-stakes game, with many of us aware of the importance of developing a secure attachment with our child whilst also finding it very difficult to do so. This can be especially true in the early days, weeks and months of parenthood when everything has changed and we are faced with a whole new human to get to know and love but who might feel pretty overwhelming for us.

The good news is that you can build and reinforce a secure bond with a child without being an all-singing, all-dancing parent. What our children need more than anything else is a quiet consistency; simply being predictably and reliably present is an important starting point.

The ideas I've shared can work well in the early weeks of parenthood but can be revisited any time that you feel unable to connect with your children in other ways and need a quieter way to continue to reinforce your bond with them.

Five Things You Could Try

1. **Just be there:** Simply reliably showing up for your child is the first step in bond-building. Being physically and, if you can, emotionally present alongside your child can be enough. There are a myriad of reasons why it might be hard to do more than this sometimes, but this can be enough. In my own parenting journey I've reverted to this tactic often. Most notably with six-month-old Ellie, fresh to us from foster care who cried continuously and wouldn't be held. I sat by her cot, just there. Nothing more, for what felt like weeks. It took time but that bond did build as she started to feel settled. A few years later, when my body was so ravaged by anorexia that I had the strength to do nothing but lie in a hospital bed, my girls got in and lay with me. I told them I loved them. I could do no more at the time, but it was enough.

   Sometimes, when we can do no more, our consistent physical presence is enough. It might be that you need to put in noise-cancelling headphones just to be able to bear to be near your crying baby, but if you can find a way to just be there, it's a good enough first step.

2. **Use routines and rituals to make small moments special:** Even the most mundane everyday tasks can turn into moments of bonding with a little bit of thought. Developing routines and

rituals to accompany tasks like feeding, nappy changing and bedtime can make these moments feel safe and familiar for children of all ages. This might mean doing things in a similar order, using the same words, singing the same song or putting on the same music or noise. You might get more adventurous and add little games into the ritual, whatever you like really, just things that add a feeling of safety and sameness. As well as creating safe, predictable moments for your child, which will aid bonding for you both, this can also make many tasks feel more manageable for you as well, as the familiar is generally less anxiety-provoking than anything new.

Sometimes as parents, we think we have to be exciting and inventive and constantly doing new things to stimulate our children, but sameness is soothing and will aid secure attachment, so find what works for you and rinse and repeat.

3. **Caring touch:** Touch builds a physical bridge between parent or carer and child, but this can feel challenging for some of us; and sometimes for our children too. Explore what feels good for you and also what your baby or child responds to well. Some children will love gentle touch or stroking. Some will like hand-holding or tickling. Others will like deep touch or hugging whilst others might simply like to feel your body curled around theirs. Notice what feels good and build more of it into your regular routines. These little moments can also be superb for co-regulation as your bodies fall in sync with one another and you both begin to feel more content and calm.

4. **Sing:** One of the best pieces of advice I was ever given as a new parent is that it's almost impossible to feel angry when you sing. Many parents and carers find themselves feeling angry or irritable with their baby, who may be the source of lack of sleep and lots of noise. We can end up feeling frustrated and helpless about how to make things better. Run-down and lacking in self-care, we're far more likely than usual to feel angry or to melt down, and this can lead to

further guilt, shame or frustration as we know that this won't help us or our baby. So, try singing. It really does work. I went for something simple – 'Twinkle, Twinkle Little Star' – whilst I paced up and down willing my baby to be quieter. You might be a little more inventive in your musical choices, but either way, you may well find that singing helps to diffuse your anger, and may help your baby to calm too, because even if you don't think you have a great voice, it will sound wonderful to your little one.

5. **Watch together:** If you're looking for ways to quietly build bridges with older children, watching something together can work well. A film, favourite TV show, a YouTube channel they're into or their favourite TikToker – let them choose and just sit calmly with them, quietly showing an interest and letting them let you into their world and the things they enjoy. When I was in recovery from my big anorexia relapse, I used to take Ellie to the cinema on a Sunday morning. All I had to do was get us there and sit in the dark with her snuggled on my knee. That was the only expectation, and to this day, watching films together always feels like a special thing for the two of us. These days, I'm learning a lot from, and about, my children by watching episodes of their favourite Netflix shows with them. It's a really easy way to show an interest which doesn't take a lot of emotional energy, but which my children seem to really appreciate.

Reflection

What's working well? What are you already doing? Could you do more of it?

....

....

....

....

What would you like to change?

....

....

....

....

What new ideas could you try?

....

....

....

....

My next tiny step is... What tiny step could you commit to taking today or tomorrow to work towards a different way of doing things?

....

....

....

....

Notes

....

....

....

....

Idea 3: Clear Expectations

Setting boundaries, role-modelling and sticking to clear expectations around day-to-day life can make things feel far safer and more predictable for both adult and child. Everyone knows where they stand, and we can develop a set of rules or expectations that work well for our family and aim to enable us to manage and thrive.

Five Things You Could Try

1. **Do it your way:** As a neurodivergent parent or carer, you may have different needs, priorities and expectations of daily life than other families. That's absolutely okay and you'll do far better working out what works for you than trying to fit your family into someone else's cookie-cutter template.

   It's also important to remember that what you think is happening in every other home, and what is actually happening, is often very different. People tend to keep very quiet about the things they are doing that don't conform to the norm; so even if you think you're the only family doing things a certain way, you're probably a lot less alone than you imagine.

2. **Pick your battles:** Pick your battles and forgive yourself for letting go of the things that might seem important to other families but feel less important to you. If your children are generally healthy and happy and safe then you're doing just fine. With less physical and emotional energy to go around than our neurotypical peers may have, we need to spend the energy we do have wisely and maybe that means having a slightly more laid-back approach to table manners or screen time. Decide what matters most to you as an individual and focus in on a consistent predictable approach to those things rather than burning yourself out trying to be a super-parent and struggling horribly with the enormity of it.

3. **Rule-make together:** The best rules are often the ones agreed as a family. Once children are old enough to begin to engage in conversations about how things work at home, it can be helpful to start to discuss the rules within the family and how things need to happen in order for everyone to stay happy and safe. Your children will feel heard, and they're more likely to adhere to rules that they've had a hand in shaping. It also gives your children a chance to help you understand what is important to them. For example, in our family we have a

'no jump scares' rule. Myself and one of my daughters both have a heightened startle response and people innocently creeping up behind us or jumping from behind a corner to say 'boo' can be enough to send either of us into a complete tailspin, so as a family we've discussed this and agreed simply not to engage in this form of fun. It might feel harmless in other families, but not in ours.

The other benefit of discussing rather than simply imposing rules is that it gives you a chance to explain your reasoning, and children are more likely to follow rules and guidance if they understand why it matters. For example, in our family we always speak one at a time. There are lots of reasons for this, but the most important is that more than one person speaking at a time can feel really overwhelming for me and my autistic daughters. Because we've discussed this, everyone understands and does their best to adhere.

4. **Role model:** Role-modelling is far more effective than rule-making in the long run. Your children learn from your every action, so thinking about what kind of behaviours, attitudes and actions you'd hope to see from your children and role-modelling those things yourself can be very powerful. If we agree rules around screen time or bedtime or mealtimes, for example, and then clearly don't value those rules enough to follow them ourselves, this sends a very strong message to our children, who are far less likely to do as we've all agreed to.

5. **Communication:** Developing clear expectations around communication can make a huge difference to our ability to cope with day-to-day life. The family environment can feel very busy and as if we are constantly bombarded with new information. Taking the time to explain to your family how much difference the way they communicate can make to how much you can take on board, as well as how you feel, can help everyone understand the importance of your expectations, so they'll try hard to stick them.

COMMUNICATION GUIDELINE SUGGESTIONS

Different people will benefit from different expectations around communication, but here are a collection of ideas from other neurodivergent parents and carers:

- We only talk one at a time.
- It is okay to be silent, we don't have to fill every gap.
- We say what we mean and we mean what we say.
- We avoid idioms; if we do use them, we explain them.
- We keep things simple.
- If someone doesn't understand, we repeat what we've said and give a moment for processing, then check understanding and rephrase if necessary.
- We try to be patient and kind in all interactions.
- We write important things down as well as saying them.
- We don't jump in to finish each other's sentences, because we all have a right to tell our own story in our own time.
- We listen with our full attention.
- We respect different points of view.
- We point out jokes and sarcasm if it's not immediately obvious.
- We use text messages to open difficult conversations (and sometimes to continue them too).
- It's okay to have hoods up or eyes down during conversations.
- No one will be forced to join in the conversation verbally, nor will they be frozen out of the conversation if they're present but quiet.
- We laugh with each other but never at each other.
- We name our feelings and express them rather than letting them stew.
- We ask directly for what we want rather than implying it.
- We are all learning all the time, so if someone doesn't understand, we patiently explain and never make them feel stupid for what they don't yet know.

- Everyone's opinion matters and should have a chance to be heard.

These represent the priorities and experiences of many different families, but there might be a handful of ideas in here that inspire you to explore how communication would best work in your home. Remember though, that none of us are perfect, so even once we've established guidelines for good communication in our family, it can be hard to stick to them. Acknowledging your aims and trying to get some of it right, some of the time, is a great starting point. Practice makes permanent, so stick at it and you'll likely find that with time, it all starts to come a little more naturally and more of your familial communications take a shape that feels comfortable and constructive for everyone.

NON-SPOKEN COMMUNICATION

In our diverse families, communication takes on various forms. Some family members may not always rely on spoken words, either because they can't speak at times or find it overwhelming. If this is true of your family, it's crucial to create an environment where non-spoken communication is not only accepted but valued, ensuring that no one feels stigmatized for how they express themselves.

Here are some ideas that can help you establish an inclusive and supportive approach to non-spoken communication within your family:

- **Acknowledge non-spoken communication:** Many of us use non-spoken methods like text messages, AAC (augmentative and alternative communication) devices or visual plans to effectively convey our thoughts and feelings. These methods are just as valid and meaningful as speaking.
- **Create a safe space for non-verbal communication:** There are moments when speech becomes challenging, overwhelming, or simply unnecessary. In such times, we wholeheartedly

embrace non-verbal communication methods. Everyone in the family understands that it's perfectly okay to use text, AAC devices, or visual cues to express themselves, and there is no judgement attached.

- **Adapt to individual needs:** Each family member is unique, and this extends to their preferred mode of communication. Some of us may rely more on non-spoken methods, and that's not just fine but commendable. We flexibly adjust our communication style to ensure that everyone can participate comfortably, regardless of the method they choose.
- **Use visual supports:** Visual aids such as schedules, Social Stories™, or picture communication systems can be incredibly helpful, especially for individuals who thrive on visual cues. These supports not only enhance communication but also contribute to a more structured and understandable environment.
- **Respect response time:** Understanding that some family members may require additional time to process information, we allow for extended response times. This patience creates a stress-free atmosphere where everyone can communicate at their own pace.
- **Establish a communication board:** A shared communication board, whether physical or digital, can serve as a central hub for family communication. It allows for messages to be conveyed efficiently, and it's a place where everyone's input is valued.

By implementing these guidelines, you ensure that your family's communication is not limited to spoken words but extends to a wide array of effective and accommodating methods. It's a reflection of your family's commitment to embracing diversity and making sure that every voice, spoken or otherwise, is heard and respected.

Reflection

What's working well? What are you already doing? Could you do more of it?

....

....

....

....

What would you like to change?

....

....

....

....

What new ideas could you try?

....

....

....

....

My next tiny step is... What tiny step could you commit to taking today or tomorrow to work towards a different way of doing things?

....

....

....

....

Notes

....

....

....

....

Idea 4: Enjoy the Child You Have

Your child is unique. Enjoy them. It can be easy to fall into the trap of competing and comparing either within families or beyond, but we will understand more than most how hard it can feel to constantly be held to the standards of others. Instead, lean into what you most love about your child and your relationship with them, and watch your relationship flourish when they are free to comfortably be themselves.

Five Things You Could Try

1. **Strengths first:** Try to consider your child through the lens of their strengths rather than any challenges they may face day to day. Introduce them this way when you talk about them to other people, even if your child isn't there to hear it. The stories adults tell about children are the stories children go on to tell about themselves. Make sure the story you tell about your child is one they'll enjoy living up to rather than one that drags them down.

2. **Jar of joy:** Keep track of the very best moments that you have with your child and revisit them regularly, especially during difficult times. An easy and very tangible way to do this is to make a note of these little moments and put them in a jar. Every now and then pick a memory out of the jar and enjoy it anew. This can be a nice thing to turn to in the more difficult moments. Other ways you might do this could be through journaling, keeping a list on your phone or taking photographs to remind you of moments of connection or joy and keeping them in an album together. I have my computer show all my favourite photographic memories as a screen saver. It is incredibly distracting and I can watch it for ages, but it fills my heart with joy.

3. **Be curious:** Your child is always growing and changing. Be curious about who they are today and never stop learning about them. Ask them questions and try to understand their opinions and how they experience the world.

4. **Do it your way:** The relationship you have with each of your children will be unique to the two of you. Notice these differences and amplify them. Rather than trying to be more like everyone else, be more just like the two of you and really enjoy what works well in the relationship, no matter how strange other people might find those things.

5. **Meaningful compliments:** Get into the habit of noticing the things you respect, love, admire and appreciate about your child and tell them. Sincere, spontaneous, specific praise and compliments feel good for our child and can contribute to healthy self-esteem. Constantly reinforcing what is great about our child leads to a much more positive experience day to day than falling into cycles of punitive nagging.

Reflection

What's working well? What are you already doing? Could you do more of it?

....

....

....

....

What would you like to change?

....

....

....

....

What new ideas could you try?

....

....

....

....

My next tiny step is... What tiny step could you commit to taking today or tomorrow to work towards a different way of doing things?

....

....

....

....

Notes

....

....

....

....

Idea 5: Be Open and Honest

I learned repeatedly from my research that openness and honesty was a real strength of many neurodivergent parents. It wasn't always seen as a strength, though, with parents and carers often noting that they felt they overshared or that they felt that their willingness to answer their children's questions and explore taboo topics set them apart from other parents, and this could feel uncomfortable. However, I strongly believe that this tendency towards openness and honesty that many of us have can be a positive part of our parenting approach if we embrace it.

Feedback from children also suggested that they often appreciated this approach:

> **'My dad is different to other dads. I can ask him anything and I know he will tell me the answer rather than fobbing me off. If he doesn't know the answer he doesn't fob me off.'**

> **'Other people's parents treat them like idiots. My mum talks straight to me. I like it.'**

'I find it helpful when my mum explains the things that she finds hard and how that feels for her. It helps me to help her and it also means I can be more honest about the things I find hard too and I know she will do her best to help me.'

Five Things You Could Try

1. **Name what you find hard:** Talking to your children about your experience as a neurodivergent adult, and the challenges that can bring, can help them to help you to navigate the world. Whilst some people are inclined to protect their children by pretending things are okay all the time, this rarely works long-term because children are astute and if we don't tell them what's wrong, they'll often imagine a far more terrible 'truth' than the actual truth.

   Exploring and explaining what helps, what doesn't and how things feel, openly and honestly, will help our children to make small changes that can help us enormously. It also creates an environment where they can be open and honest in return and enable us to understand and respond to their experience of the world.

2. **Learn out loud:** Let your child see you learning. Rather than sharing the end result with them, let them see the process and the different things you tried along the way. Children seeing parents or carers problem-solving, help-seeking and dusting themselves off and trying again is far stronger role-modelling than children observing adults who appear to serenely glide through life always getting things right first time, as this can feel like an unobtainable standard and can make those adults feel unapproachable.

   I try to practise this every day, but it's never more obvious than when I'm at the climbing wall with Ellie. Ellie has become very bold and adventurous in her climbing, often repeatedly trying climbs that are right at the limits of her capabilities on which she might take numerous falls before she makes progress. I'm proud to see her climb like this as she hasn't always. She used to climb well within her capabilities, which limited her progress and enjoyment. This changed when instead of simply coaching her, I started climbing my own projects alongside hers. This means that Ellie now gets to see (and contribute to) the process of me figuring out how to master climbs that I find challenging. She watches and helps me route-plan, problem-solve and test out a whole bunch of ideas about how to complete a tricky climb. Most of all, she gets to see me repeatedly fail, fall and try again. Every time I see her take a fall and run back to the wall with a smile on her face ready to try something new or try a bit harder I feel a burst of pride.

3. **Problem-solve together:** Problem-solving with a child or as a whole family can provide a non-judgemental environment for exploring the problems or challenges a family member is facing. The process of exploring different ideas together and sharing past experiences where every voice is equally heard can be a great way both to solve the problem in hand and also to build bonds. This can apply to any problem at all, but I have personally found it especially helpful to explore friendship issues as a family. My teenage daughters can offer a lot of insight here and I learn a lot from them.

4. **Make it okay to make mistakes:** We all make mistakes all the time and they are an important vehicle for learning, so making it okay to make, share and learn from our mistakes as a family can be a gift to every single family member. We can do this by role-modelling sharing our own mistakes and what we've learned from them, or problem-solving with family how to do things differently next time. You could also make a ritual out of it, like one of the families I was working with:

   > **'Every evening we share a fail of the day. We talk about something we got wrong and what we learned from it. Sometimes it gets really deep, other days it's hilarious!'**

5. **Love out loud:** In addition to being open and honest about

challenges and mistakes, we can also aim to be more open and honest about our love for our children. Our love can feel so big that it seems impossible that our children wouldn't know that we love them, but sometimes they don't, and they need to have it spelt out for them. Children, especially those with low self-esteem, hugely benefit from regularly having all the things we love about them clearly communicated.

DIFFERENT WAYS TO LOVE OUT LOUD

There are many ways to say, 'I love you,' and many of them don't involve saying anything at all. Different things work for different families and for children of different ages. Here are some of the ways that families in our community shared their love with their children:

- He rolls his eyes when I say it out loud so I've taken to texting him.
- I write postcards to my kids telling them things I love about them or that I'm proud of.
- Cuddles and kisses work best for us. I keep thinking they'll grow out of them, but they never seem to.
- We have a special handshake that ends with a kiss and a cuddle – it's a funny little ritual but it really works for us.
- We mostly use emojis, which seems a more acceptable way for a teen to be told they are loved and to tell me in return.
- It can be easy to become a nag, so I now try for every nag, to tell my son three 'nices'. It reminds me, and him, that he's a great kid.
- I tell her in the car when we're side by side and there's no one to hear so she doesn't feel embarrassed. It also means she has space to really hear what I've said, which is important because what I've said really matters.
- We walk hand in hand and I try to tell her all the time. I don't remember ever being told I was loved as a child so I try to tell my daughter often.

Reflection

What's working well? What are you already doing? Could you do more of it?

....

....

....

....

What would you like to change?

....

....

....

....

What new ideas could you try?

....

....

....

....

My next tiny step is... What tiny step could you commit to taking today or tomorrow to work towards a different way of doing things?

....

....

....

....

Notes

....

....

....

....

Idea 6: Have One-to-One Time

Focusing on one person at a time can make it feel far more possible for us to develop meaningful relationships and manage those developing relationships whilst also coping with our own sensory and emotional needs. One-to-one time is easier to manage because we've only got to cater to two sets of needs so it involves far less compromise. It also lends itself to development of a far deeper relationship than can happen in bigger groups as we can focus ourselves entirely on the child we've chosen to spend time with today.

Quality, rather than quantity, is important here. Even a few snatched minutes together with a child can meaningfully contribute to the development of your relationship if you're fully present during those minutes. Quite how you choose to spend that time depends on what feels possible and enjoyable for you and the particular child, but I've shared a few ideas to help get you thinking.

Five Things You Could Try

1. **Hobby together:** Is there a hobby that both you and your child enjoy that you could spend time doing together? Otherwise could they join you in something you enjoy, or would they be happy to invite you into the world of one of their hobbies? Or perhaps there is something new you could both take up together?

   Having an activity that you can regularly enjoy doing alongside your child can create an opportunity to regularly spend time together in a way that might feel more structured and less intimidating than unscripted time. It can be rewarding and connecting to develop skills together too. It's also great role-modelling for your child to see you in the role of learner, and can feel great for them to step into the role of teacher sometimes too. You don't need to be good at stuff for this idea to work, you simply need to be prepared to give it a go.

2. **Schedule a one-to-one 'appointment':** This is about quality one-to-one time with your child rather than just passing time in their company. It can help to approach it as you might a work meeting and actually diarize it. It doesn't need to be a long meeting, but making a commitment to both yourself and your child that 'on Saturday at 4 p.m. we'll take half an hour together' will make it feel unambiguous, and it is something your child is likely to look forward to. Try to schedule this time at points in the day and the week when you tend to feel relatively calm and happy, so you can enjoy this time and it doesn't become an extra stressor.

3. **Be fully present during routine moments:** Conversely, rather than making a special appointment, you can take a look at your daily and weekly routines and see whether there are any moments when you are regularly in the company of your child, which you can turn into opportunities for short bursts of quality time. Perhaps as you walk your child to school, you'll fully engage in being with them rather than engaging with the to-do list in your head. Maybe the drive home from football practice on a Wednesday is a good time to talk to your daughter, or you could decide to add a bedtime story back into the evening routine with your son. There are all sorts of potential opportunities if you look for them, and these can act like microdoses of relationship-building and can prove healthy for your bond with your child over time.

4. **Take an interest in their interests:** Invite your child to invite you into their world. Perhaps they have a deep interest or hobby or passion that they invest a lot of their time and energy into that isn't something you understand or especially care about. Set aside a few minutes to ask them to talk to you or show you what interests them and leap in. Allow them to take on the mantel of expert and try to be curious and non-judgemental.

   This might mean anything from watching their favourite YouTube channel and asking them to explain the in-jokes to you, to asking them to explain to you a bit about their favourite video game while they show you how to play (and perhaps have a laugh whilst you try to have a go – it's always harder than it looks). Or maybe they'd be happy to help you take your first baby steps on a skateboard, or would enjoy telling you exactly why you need to take more interest in climate change. Whatever it is that your child chooses to spend their time doing, taking an interest in it and asking them to tell you, show you or guide you can be a brilliant way to learn a little more about your child and to make them feel truly seen and heard by you.

5. **Have a child-led day:** This one takes real bravery and isn't one I've ever felt able to commit to myself... yet... But I have seen it work brilliantly for others. The idea is that you commit to spending a day with your child, just the two of you, and they get to completely set the agenda, from where you'll go and how you'll get there to what you'll do, what you'll eat, and so on. The potential unknown element of this would prove too much for me and a whole day feels like a long time to be out of control of things, so I think accommodations I'd make for myself would be allowing my child to be in charge, but asking them to plan ahead, at least a little, and perhaps limiting it to half a day.

IDEAS FOR CHILD-DIRECTED ONE-TO-ONE TIME

Things that have worked well in our house that are similar to a child-led day but that don't involve quite so fully relinquishing control include:

- **One-to-one holidays:** I gave both girls a list of options I'd be happy to do and they picked from the list. Ellie opted for a few days of adventure at PGL (an outdoor activity centre) whilst Lyra and I learnt to surf in Wales.
- **Child in charge:** This has also worked well for travel training my autistic daughters. If one of them wants to go to Brighton, which is a nearby town for us, it becomes their responsibility

to manage details like when we need to leave, what bus we're catching there, buying the tickets, navigating us the other end, picking somewhere for lunch, ordering, and so on. This builds their skills, gives them a say in the agenda and relieves me of some of the tasks I find most stressful.

- **Bucket list:** My children having a bucket list of activities that they want to do gives me a starting point that I can pick and choose from. I've been surprised by how little and doable the things on my daughters' lists sometimes are, and how much joy it's easy to create by doing something on their list. They're often things I'd enjoy in the right moment too, such as ice cream by the sea or paddleboarding at our favourite spot.

Reflection

What's working well? What are you already doing? Could you do more of it?

....

....

....

....

What would you like to change?

....

....

....

....

What new ideas could you try?

....

....

....

....

My next tiny step is... What tiny step could you commit to taking today or tomorrow to work towards a different way of doing things?

....

....

....

....

Idea 7: Take Time for You so You Can Enjoy Time with Them

It's hard to enjoy time with our children if we haven't first made enough time for ourselves. Whilst we tend to put our own needs and wants at the bottom of our priority list, it's always worth remembering that we're better able to be the parent our children want and need when we look after ourselves. When we're better rested and regulated we can be more fun, more imaginative and more consistently calm, kind and loving.

Five Things You Could Try

1. **Balance the diary:** As a parent or carer, it's very easy to put everyone else's needs constantly before your own. There are no prizes for this, though, and it's a sure-fire route to burnout. Instead, try to balance your diary, specifically noticing when there are particular family items that are likely to take their toll on you and try to schedule even a small amount of solo time to counterbalance this.

   Regularly check the diary and try to keep it in balance. I appreciate this might sound unrealistic, and you probably feel like you don't have time, but a small investment of solo time now could save you from weeks of burnout later.

2. **Plan family-time breaks:** Actually planning how you can fit short bursts of solo time within family time can make things feel more manageable. I find this especially important

on days out or holidays. This might just be a few minutes and involve a little forward planning or discussion with the other people who you'll be there with. For example, if you've headed out for the day with your family to a farm with a play barn, perhaps you can plan ahead to leave another adult in charge whilst the kids run around the play barn for a few minutes and you go and take a quiet walk to reset and recharge.

I always take headphones and a book with me wherever I go, so I can take emergency me-time if I need to. Knowing I can do this often makes it more possible not to, though there have been many an occasion when I've been very glad of my emergency book.

3. **Take a dose of quiet ahead of family activities:** A short amount of quiet alone time immediately ahead of intense family activity can really increase our ability to cope and manage. During the alone time, we can focus on getting ourselves to a good, calm, emotionally regulated place which will mean that our capacity to manage what comes next increases a little. It doesn't need to be long, but getting in the habit of spending even five minutes between preparing for and jumping into family time can be a game changer.

4. **Build solo escape tasks into your daily routine:** Have a think about the things you do every day and consider whether any of them could be developed into a solo escape task where you focus in on yourself and get to a place of peace and calm before continuing with your day. For example, perhaps you give yourself permission to put on a favourite song to sing along to as you load the dishwasher rather than using this time to run through the never-ending to-do list in your head.

5. **Relish the early mornings or late evenings:** You may find it easiest to find a little alone time in the bookends of the day. I love the hours before the rest of my family are awake – in fact, I'm writing this in the wee small hours of the morning

whilst the rest of the house sleeps, and I'm blissfully alone in a very quiet house. The end of the day can work too. Taking just a few minutes to yourself once the day is done can also help you transition towards bedtime better as you'll be more relaxed as you start thinking about going to sleep.

Reflection

What's working well? What are you already doing? Could you do more of it?

....

....

....

....

What would you like to change?

....

....

....

....

What new ideas could you try?

....

....

....

....

My next tiny step is... What tiny step could you commit to taking today or tomorrow to work towards a different way of doing things?

....

....

....

....

Notes

....

....

....

....

Idea 8: Listen

Listening well is a skill that can form the bedrock of positive relationships with both adults and children. People love to feel listened to and that they've been seen, heard and understood by someone else, so these skills can be applied elsewhere in your life too. As someone who likes a clearly defined set of rules, I love the fact that listening is something where there are a few simple steps I can follow to do it well. The other great thing is that if you're someone who can find it harder to contribute to conversations, making a few tweaks to your listening can make this go unnoticed as many people of all ages love the chance to talk about themselves and your near silence often won't even register.

Five Things You Could Try

1. **Focus:** Make this conversation right now the most important thing in your world. Close all open brain tabs and put screens to one side. Be wholly there to hear your child for just a few minutes.
2. **Walk and talk:** Walking alongside your child can make the conversation flow, especially if it's a trickier one as it removes the pressure that sitting face to face can bring. Additionally, walking will help both of you regulate, and it allows the conversation to slow down without a hurry to fill every single gap.
3. **Ask open questions:** Questions that require a deeper answer will enable your child to explore and express what's going on for them. You can also ask little prompts to encourage them to go further still with their answers.

PROMPTS TO ENCOURAGE DEEPER CONVERSATION

A few words is all it takes to encourage your child to keep hold of the conversational baton and dive more deeply into whatever it is they're talking about. Rather than strict turn taking, allow them to take extra turns in the conversation whilst you remain in the role of listener.

Some of my favourites prompts to encourage conversational depth include:

- Tell me more...
- Keep going...
- How did that make you feel? (I know it's terribly clichéd but it works.)
- What would a friend say?
- Why do you think she did that?
- What happened next?
- What surprised you?
- What helped?
- What made things worse?
- What do you want to happen?
- What do you think he thought about that?
- What led up to this?

These prompts don't only work for children. I find similar prompts to be incredibly helpful in adult social situations when I'm struggling to talk a lot. It turns out that most people love to talk about themselves and will feel like they've had a really good conversation if they do 95 per cent of the talking. You can enable this with just a few prompts and it means you don't have to do lots of talking if you don't want to or it feels too hard right now.

4. **Reflect and check:** Summarizing what you've just heard in your own words and saying it back to your child actively demonstrates that you've been listening and creates

a chance for them to correct any misunderstanding on your part.

5. **Stay silent:** Sometimes, the best thing to say is nothing at all. If you keep quiet, your child will often fill the gap. I sometimes glance at my watch and decide I'm going to allow a full minute to pass before I next speak. This can help prevent the urge to jump in after only a few seconds.

Reflection

What's working well? What are you already doing? Could you do more of it?

....

....

....

....

What would you like to change?

....

....

....

....

What new ideas could you try?

....

....

....

....

My next tiny step is... What tiny step could you commit to taking today or tomorrow to work towards a different way of doing things?

....

....

....

....

Notes

....

....

....

....

Idea 9: Lean into Fun

Fun and laughter are great ways to build relationships with our children. True fun and laughter happen only when we feel safe and connected so I often consider them as symptoms of a healthy relationship. What we consider fun may be quite different than our neurotypical peers, and that's okay. Just remember to lean into the right kind of fun for you and your family and don't beat yourself up for not achieving picture-perfect smiles and laughter doing standard stuff.

Five Things You Could Try

1. **Embrace your inner child:** Little kids tend to be fun-seeking, but that tendency diminishes with age. Many of us have less fun once adult responsibilities take over and many activities begin to be seen as 'childish', or we start to feel that our activities should serve a purpose beyond fun.

   What if we specifically engaged with activities that sparked a little joy regardless of their typical age range or their utility? Why not jump on the swings in the park, or paddle in the sea or fly that kite or any one of a number of things each day that we might feel too grown up to do? If you're curious or you think you'd enjoy it, do it. Developing your sense of fun and playfulness can help you bridge the adult–child divide as you start to be able to empathize more with your children's world, and create moments for laughter and connection.

2. **Let laughter grow:** When laughter happens we have a choice; we can either stifle it and move on or we can allow the laughter to grow and embrace it. Unless it feels totally inappropriate to do so, I'd advocate leaning in and laughing hard whenever you get the chance. It feels GOOD and it's an instant relationship boost for you and whoever you're with at the time.

3. **Write a bucket list:** Write a bucket list with your kids of things you'd all enjoy doing and commit to trying to work through it over the next few weeks. This can help to plan and control the fun if that's what you need (I do), and also gives you a chance to think together about what you'd all enjoy.

   The list doesn't have to be full of big things. A great place to start might be reflecting on times you've had fun as a family in the past. My daughters' current list (written without my input) includes:

   - water fight
   - picnic on the downs
   - swimming in the sea
   - homemade bubble tea
   - ride a roller coaster
   - BBQ and garden games
   - ice cream on the beach
   - Mario Kart Championship
   - day at the zoo.

4. **Try saying yes more:** Sometimes it can feel like our job as a parent or carer is to be the killer of joy. 'No' can feel like our most uttered word as we try to keep things sensible and tidy and as they should be. What if we tried to say yes a little more and embraced fun and laughter when it tried to evolve? Try to catch yourself about to say no – and say yes instead and watch what happens. My most recent example was the girls wanting to paddle in the sea. We had not planned to and I had no towels or change of clothes and was on the verge of saying no. I'm so glad I didn't as watching the girls lark

about in the water laughing their heads off and seeing their smiles when they were done was brilliant and the lack of a towel felt inconsequential.

5. **Join in:** As adults, we often create opportunities for fun for our children and then stand by the sidelines. If, instead, we join in sometimes, we create opportunities for bond-building with our children and fun for ourselves. Kick a ball, paint a pot, clamber on the climbing frame or game alongside... There are opportunities to join in with fun stuff with our kids all the time, we just have to take the chance.

Reflection

What's working well? What are you already doing? Could you do more of it?

....

....

....

....

What would you like to change?

....

....

....

....

What new ideas could you try?

....

....

....

....

My next tiny step is... What tiny step could you commit to taking today or tomorrow to work towards a different way of doing things?

....

....

....

....

Notes

....

....

....

....

Idea 10: Forgive the Ruptures and Focus on Repair

There's no doubt about it, things will go wrong sometimes and there will be moments when you're not able to be the parent or carer you'd like to be. Especially if they're messy or explosive, these moments can lead to a great deal of guilt or shame. They're a part of parenting that can feel unique to us as people don't tend to share the ugly bits of their parenting journey with the rest of the world. Rest assured though, you're not alone; just this week my response to a child leaving my coat out in the rain after making a den with it was not quite as I'd have hoped. On a good day, I'd like to think I'd have encouraged the outdoor adventure and ingenuity in using a range of different items to create the den whilst perhaps suggesting that taking care of other people's possessions was worth considering. On this day I totally lost it. Like, REALLY lost it. I screamed like a banshee, pretty much made my children think they were the worst humans alive ever for daring to touch my things, then I stormed off in the manner of a three-year-old slamming every door I passed through before hiding under the covers in my bed in a seething, crying mess. It wasn't pretty and certainly not an example I'd hold up as perfect parenting.

But it happens, and we can either beat ourselves up about it, or we can pick ourselves up and use it as a chance to role-model to our children how to repair ruptures. These are lessons that will last them a lifetime, so even the stormiest cloud can have a silver lining.

Sometimes, as parents, we experience moments of intense stress and overwhelm (it's not just you). These moments, often referred to as 'meltdowns', can happen to anyone but may be more frequent for autistic/ADHD parents due to sensory sensitivities and the challenges of navigating a neurotypical world (more on meltdowns in Chapter 9). In my case, the sight of my coat left out in the rain triggered an autistic stress reaction. The wet coat made the day feel unpredictable and chaotic, which was distressing for me, and the sensory stress compounded this. The feeling of wetness and discomfort from the soaked coat intensified the overwhelm. It's crucial for both parents and children to understand that these reactions are not a reflection of bad parenting but a response to a challenging situation.

Five Things You Could Try

1. **Say sorry:** 'Sorry' is one of the most powerful words a child can hear from an adult they trust and respect. It's not a word kids are used to hearing from adults and we would do well to say it more. Acknowledge your mistake, own it and apologize for it.

2. **Revisit the rupture at a time of calm:** Some time later once you're all in a calmer, happier frame of mind, it's time to revisit the scene of the crime with your children. Wait until you're all emotionally regulated because our thinking-speaking brains go offline when we're angry or anxious.

3. **Be curious:** Explore what happened with your children. Reflect on the situation with a spirit of curiosity, wondering what led

you to feel and act in those ways and wondering aloud what might make a difference another time. This is brave, brilliant role-modelling for your children who'll see you owning the issue and proactively considering how to make things feel different in future.

4. **Forgive:** If you get stuff wrong, it's important to forgive yourself. It's also helpful to try to forgive anyone or anything that triggered the rupture. Voicing your forgiveness aloud can be deeply reassuring to your children. As adults, if we regularly try to lovingly forgive our children when they make mistakes, they, in turn, will learn to be forgiving of our mistakes and misdemeanours.

5. **Move on:** Once you've got calm and curious and you've forgiven one another, it's time to consign this moment to history. No good comes from continually revisiting difficult moments. Once we've learned what we can, it's time to completely move on. Everyone, adults and children alike, deserves regular opportunities for a fresh start and today's mistakes should certainly never sour tomorrow if you can possibly help it.

Reflection

What's working well? What are you already doing? Could you do more of it?

....

....

....

....

What would you like to change?

....

....

....

....

What new ideas could you try?

....

....

....

....

My next tiny step is... What tiny step could you commit to taking today or tomorrow to work towards a different way of doing things?

....

....

....

....

Notes

....

....

....

....

What Do Our Children Think?

It can be interesting to hear our children's points of view so when researching this book, some of the children of neurodivergent parents and carers were kind enough to share their thoughts. Here's what they had to say on this topic:

> 'My dad is not like other people's dads. I think he's better. Some days he is really happy and funny and we play a lot of games. Some days he is more serious and sad and he can't really play. Other people's dads are just a little bit boring all of the time. My dad is not like that.'

> 'My mum is very honest with me, instead of just telling me what I

want to hear or trying to build my self-esteem. It means I can always trust her and that when she tells me something positive, I know she totally means it.'

'I like it that I can ask her anything and she will always give me an answer or help me find one if she doesn't know.'

'I wouldn't change one single thing about my mum.'

'I love it when we get to spend time just the two of us. That feels really special.'

'My dad is a brilliant listener. He cares so much about what you're saying and he doesn't interrupt you or tell you to hurry up.'

'ADHD is a great thing for a dad to have because it means he has all these wacky ideas and so much energy. My mum gets frustrated at the mess and sometimes will be like "What's the next crazy scheme," but we have so much fun.'

'My mum understands me better than anyone because she is like me. Because she didn't know she was autistic until we found out I was, we have been learning about it together. There are so many things we have in common that we never realized before.'

'I have had a lot of foster carers. One of my current foster carers is autistic and ADHD, like me. He's the first person I've felt comfortable with and understood by in a very long time. I never feel like he's judging me and I always feel like he's doing his best to help me, when other people might get angry or give up.'

Summary

To wrap up, here's a quick reference summary of the ideas shared in this chapter.

Idea 1: Embrace Being a Successful Neurodivergent Parent, Not a Failed Neurotypical One

Embrace your unique parenting style as a neurodivergent

individual, recognizing that it may differ from the norm, but that doesn't make it any less successful; in fact, it can be a source of strength and innovation.

Idea 2: Bond Quietly

Bonding with your child doesn't require elaborate gestures; quiet consistency, routines, caring touch, singing and watching together can help strengthen your connection, especially in the early days of parenthood.

Idea 3: Clear Expectations

Establishing clear expectations, tailored to your family's unique needs, fosters predictability and harmony. Consider involving your children in rule-making, modelling desired behaviours and creating effective communication guidelines to enhance your family's daily life.

Idea 4: Enjoy the Child You Have

Celebrate your child's strengths and unique qualities rather than constantly comparing them to others. Create a jar of joyful memories, be curious about their evolving personality, embrace the uniqueness of your relationship with each child, and offer meaningful compliments to boost their self-esteem.

Idea 5: Be Open and Honest

Embrace openness and honesty in your parenting approach. Discuss your neurodivergent experiences with your child, share challenges and feelings openly, and create an environment where your child can be open and honest in return. Encourage mutual understanding and support within your family.

Idea 6: Have One-to-One Time

Focusing on one child at a time can strengthen your relationships with them. Quality one-to-one time, even in short bursts, can make a meaningful impact. Engage in shared hobbies, schedule one-to-one time, be present during routine moments, take an interest in their passions, or even have child-led days to deepen your connections.

Idea 7: Take Time for You

Prioritize self-care to be the best parent for your child. Balance your schedule, plan solo breaks during family activities, incorporate moments of quiet into your daily routine, and cherish early mornings or late evenings as opportunities for personal time and relaxation.

Idea 8: Listen

Listening attentively is a fundamental skill for building positive relationships. Focus on the conversation, ask open questions, walk and talk to ease communication, reflect and check for understanding. And sometimes, staying silent can encourage your child to share more.

Idea 9: Lean into Fun

Fun and laughter are essential for healthy relationships. Embrace activities that spark joy, let laughter grow naturally, create a bucket list of enjoyable experiences, try saying yes more often, and actively join in the fun with your children to strengthen your connections.

Idea 10: Forgive the Ruptures and Focus on Repair

Mistakes and ruptures are inevitable in parenting. Apologize when you make mistakes, revisit the situation when everyone is calm, be curious about what happened, practise forgiveness, and then move on. This teaches your children valuable lessons in repairing relationships and moving forward positively.

CHAPTER 3

Quick Read: Managing Your Relationship with a Parenting Partner

Having someone to parent alongside can be a fortunate position to be in because it can lighten both the physical and emotional load when you're able to parent as a team. However, loving and living with someone does not come without challenges. This is true for our neurotypical peers, so for those of us who feel like the rest of the world has read the playbook on relationships whilst we're left winging it, it's especially complicated.

Many people were quick to share that maintaining their relationships with other adults (not just their partner) was a weakness for them, but on reflection, the community had great ideas to share here. It is, perhaps, worth reflecting on your own relationships that are working better within your own life and wondering why. What is going right there and are there any lessons you could apply to other relationships?

Here's the advice the community had to share when it came to managing a relationship with a parenting partner:

- **Be honest:** Be open about any limitations if you feel comfortable. Being open and honest about your own limitations can significantly improve your relationships with parenting partners or other adults involved in your child's life.

  For example, say you have a parenting partner who often schedules last-minute meetings or activities related to your child without considering your work commitments or the challenges you face with change of routine. Instead of keeping your frustration to yourself, you could be honest about your limitations, telling your parenting partner it would be helpful to plan these activities together a bit earlier so you can be available and fully present.

By openly communicating your needs and limitations, you provide an opportunity for a constructive discussion. Most people are willing to adjust and cooperate when they understand each other's perspectives and constraints.

- **Curiosity and communication:** Our son's diagnosis is what made me realize I was autistic. Learning about what autism meant for our son enabled my husband to understand me more. I have been able to share my understanding of how things are for my son to enable my husband to get it.
- **Have clear roles:** I find it much easier to define what our roles are going to be and to be left alone to do my share without anyone around. I like to do the tidying and organizing around the house but I need space to do this without interruptions, so I can slot into my hyper-focus mode and work through the disorder and chaos methodically.
- **Share the load:** I like to make sure the share of parenting tasks is equal because I find parenting on top of full-time work very overstimulating. I am a better parent if the mental load is shared fairly. This doesn't mean everything has to be split down the middle exactly every day, it just needs to feel fair and not like it's all landing on one person all day every day.
- **Assume your parenting partner is neurodivergent:** Neurodivergent people flock together so, even if it's not been acknowledged or diagnosed, it's possible that your partner is a little neurospicy. You don't have to make a big deal of this, but you can use what you know to ensure their needs as well as your own are accommodated, such as some quiet, child-free time each day for each parent whenever possible.
- **Be adaptable and play to your strengths:** My husband has a lot of anxiety around cooking so we buy recipe boxes which he responds to really well, because each ingredient is

measured out in advance and the instructions are laid out clearly with photographs. I have ADHD so I am not keen on following instructions. I think playing to your strengths has the best outcome for children, along with asking for your needs to be met.

- **Be 'on the same page' wherever possible:** If you aren't then the child needs one of you to be the advocate and 'translator' for the other.
- **Acknowledge and work with differing viewpoints:** One area we differ on is rules. I am happier when they're clear and black and white. My husband allows for more flexibility. This can mean I feel undermined sometimes. Knowing now that I'm autistic has helped us both learn a bit about how to manage this. I try hard to let go and leave it to my husband more.
- **Remember you are partners as well as parents:** Make sure you have time and space to breathe. Remember that being in a relationship is one of the hardest things you will ever do; you have to work hard at it every day. We focus so hard on how to be a good parent, and sometimes that means we neglect working hard on being a good partner too. Being able to have open, honest discussions with your partner about what you can expect of each other, how you can best work together and the steps you can take to most enjoy one another's companionship can help you become better partners and parents.
- **Make time for date nights:** Or date days, or date hours or whatever works for you. Just try to carve out a little from the busyness and stress of family life to spend a little time one-to-one with your partner doing the kinds of things you used to enjoy before you had children.

  My mother-in-law offered to mind the baby once a week so we could take a little time together. She said that even though our baby was tiny now, one day she would grow up and move away and then it would be just the two of us left together again, and that we should take steps now to make sure that our relationship remained strong, happy and comfortable. I got the impression she was trying to prevent us from making the same mistakes she had. It was great advice for the long term and also gives us great respite now. Each week we have a window of time to have a little fun, let our hair down or simply have a really good rest.

- **How you were parented will impact on your experience of parenting:** If you are neurodivergent and your partner is not (or even if they are), you may have very different experiences of being parented and very different expectations of what parenting will look like. Sometimes a minor disagreement can bring up quite painful memories unexpectedly, and it's important not to blame that on your partner, and to try to explain and somewhat separate your emotional reaction to the past from deciding the best thing to do now.

  Usually, a pause and a chat will allow things to progress constructively. In the end, you both want the same thing (happy kind kids), and it's okay to have different views on how to get there, and to compromise, learn from experience and adjust your approach as you grow and learn together.

  In the end, I think children can benefit from the wisdom of two parents who don't always agree, as long as those disagreements are handled constructively and with mutual respect for each other's views and experiences.

In this chapter, we've explored the complexities of parenting together and collaborating with other adults involved in your child's life. It's clear that these relationships come with their unique challenges, especially for those of us navigating neurodivergence. However, within our community, we've discovered valuable insights and strategies for fostering healthier connections.

YOUR TURN

As you engage with the 'Your Turn' reflection activities, consider your own experiences with parenting together – both the challenges and successes. Reflect on the importance of honesty, the benefits of playing to your strengths, and the significance of nurturing your partnership. By learning from these experiences and insights, you can work towards creating a more harmonious and balanced parenting journey.

Reflect on your own experiences of parenting together or collaborating with other adults involved in your child's life. Have you encountered any challenges or had moments of success in these relationships? Share a specific example that stands out to you.

....

....

....

....

Consider the importance of honesty in parenting together. Have you ever found it difficult to express your needs or limitations to a co-parent or another adult involved in your child's life? How might open and honest communication benefit these relationships?

....

....

....

....

Explore the idea of assuming that your co-parent or partner may also be neurodivergent. How might this perspective influence your interactions and decisions within your shared parenting responsibilities?

....

....

Reflect on the concept of playing to your strengths as co-parents. Are there specific roles or tasks that each of you naturally excels at? How can you utilize your strengths to create a more harmonious and balanced parenting partnership?

Think about the advice on making time for date nights or quality one-on-one time with your partner. How do you currently prioritize your relationship amid the demands of parenting? What small steps can you take to nurture your connection and maintain a strong partnership?

CHAPTER 4

Quick Read: Building a Support Network

Developing a good support network can be the difference between managing and not managing. Having good support around us, whether that's formal or informal, can help us in our day-to-day lives as neurodivergent adults and can also help us to provide our children with the support they need. It's very common for neurodivergent adults to have neurodivergent children. So some of the ideas the community shared, which I draw out here, about building a support network are geared specifically towards helping us to meet the needs of children with special needs.

Remember that not all of these ideas will work for everyone; there was a great deal of diversity within the community who contributed to this book, so read through these tips that they shared, and consider which feel appealing and possible to you rather than beating yourself up for any that feel out of reach.

- **Find a local group:** It's scary, but find local groups to build up to going to. Being with other parents in similar positions is incredibly helpful. Reach out to local special needs groups. Use parent–peer support groups. Find your tribe, like-minded parents who can relate to and empathize with your situation. (There were mixed feelings about these groups amongst the community. Some people loved them, but some had found both online and offline groups to be a negative experience. The best advice I can give here is to arrive with an open mind, but don't feel obliged to persevere if it's not helping. Not all groups help all people – we're all different.)

- **Join a local online forum:** Join local online forums for parents. Be active in posting and responding to others.
- **Find your tribe online:** I have found that the online neurodivergent community is what works best for me. I'm sure there are groups around that meet face to face, but that in itself is a barrier for me.
- **Reflect on your existing connections:** I'm working hard to accept that, whilst I don't have friends who are always popping in and meeting up regularly, I do have strong friends I can rely on when needed. I consider a good friend to be someone whose door I could knock on at 3 a.m. and who would take me in, no questions asked. When I think that way, it helps me understand my support network and prevents me feeling lonely.
- **Allow yourself to be supported:** I was determined to do it all myself and I felt very lonely doing so, but I was surrounded by people happy to help me – my in-laws, people at church, people I walk my dog with. When I opened myself up to the possibility of being supported by others, that support was willingly given, whether it was just a listening ear or more practical support. Allowing myself to be supported was the biggest hurdle to overcome. I'm happier and a better parent now I've taken that leap.
- **Your children's friends' parents:** Get to know your child's friends' parents. Your child will find 'their people' and their parents often will be 'your people'.
- **Be vulnerable:** Learn that vulnerability is okay and you can find a safe place to learn to be able to be vulnerable enough to take down the mask, be seen and accepted. And that acceptance of yourself, and the stage of the journey you are in, is okay. Wherever you are at.
- **Forgive yourself:** Self-acceptance and forgiveness is so important, because parenting from a place of fear,

self-loathing and self-blame will not make it easy to bring balance and calm. Try to forgive yourself, meet the feelings (whatever they are) and share them. Even if one person knows where you're at and can support without judgement or blame, that feeling of validation you get and being able to lay those feelings down helps you to process and accept yourself and the situation.

- **Coffee mornings at school:** Having regular breakfast coffees with a group of parents/carers to share concerns about our kids coping in school was a great help. We had a wonderful head teacher, openly listening as mental and emotional needs consumed increasing amounts of time.
- **Seek others at a similar point in the journey:** Parents are at different stages in their journey. Lots of us are neurodivergent aware and positive about our own differences. Others are very much still 'in the closet', seeing autism as a condition which needs to be treated, or perhaps not recognizing their own neurodivergence. It's important that you understand where you are in this conversation so that you can support others, understand, and find your own 'tribe'.

As we wrap up this chapter on building a support network, we've delved into the importance of connecting with others who can understand and empathize with the unique challenges neurodivergent parents face. A strong support network can be a lifeline in our journey, offering insights, empathy and a sense of belonging.

YOUR TURN

As you engage with the 'Your Turn' reflection activities, take a moment to reflect on your current support network – whether it includes local groups, online forums or trusted friends. Consider the benefits of finding your tribe, allowing yourself to be supported, embracing vulnerability, and connecting with others at similar points in their parenting journey. Your experiences and insights can help you navigate the path of neurodivergent parenting with resilience and strength.

Reflect on your current support network. Are there any local groups or online forums you've already connected with to seek support and share experiences as a neurodivergent parent or caregiver? What has been your experience with these communities?

....

....

....

....

Consider the idea of finding your tribe either locally or online. Have you explored the possibility of joining groups or forums where you can connect with like-minded parents facing similar challenges? Share your thoughts on the benefits of such connections.

....

....

....

....

Reflect on the concept of allowing yourself to be supported. Have you ever felt hesitant to accept help from others or open up about your struggles? How did it feel when you eventually allowed yourself to receive support? Share any positive experiences or insights.

....

....

....

....

Think about the importance of vulnerability in building a support network. Have you ever found it challenging to be vulnerable and share your true feelings and experiences with others? How can embracing vulnerability lead to greater acceptance and understanding within your support network?

....

....

....

....

Explore the idea of seeking others who are at a similar point in their journey as parents or caregivers. Are there parents in your network who are at different stages of acceptance and understanding regarding neurodivergence? How can you navigate these differences to provide support and find your own tribe?

....

....

....

....

CHAPTER 5

Quick Read: Building New and Old Friendships

Making friends can be challenging, and for many of us, enough of the right kinds of friends can make a huge difference to our day-to-day engagement with and enjoyment of life. When sharing ideas about building and nurturing friendships, one of the community members said, 'Friendship saves lives and heals so many wounds and keeps us strong.' Which I think is a beautiful summary.

The funny thing I found about becoming a parent was that it's the time when you most need your friends because it's hard and you're facing a lot of changes, but it's a point in your life when you have the least time for friends (because it's hard and you're facing a lot of changes...). Finding ways to make and keep the kinds of friends you need now can make a huge difference to your experience of parenting. It can feel lonely, isolating and sometimes scary, or it can be a journey that is enjoyed with others who can help you figure out the best way around or over obstacles and challenges. The right kinds of friends can also provide great respite from the demands of parenting too; this can often enable us to return refreshed and better able to parent than before. I'm always very grateful for my paragliding friends who I can have fun with out on the hill and flying together. Spending time away from work and home and indulging in my hobby, nature and people I enjoy leaves me refreshed and better able to be the parent my children need.

Lots of ideas were shared by the community for making friends and building positive relationships. I hope some of these ideas will help you.

- **Be upfront:** Be honest with others about who you are and what you can and cannot commit to as a 'friend' or 'network'. For example, tell people that you cannot be in large groups or that you can only manage two hours when meeting up. Being upfront in this way has helped me find the best of friends as they know what to expect. If they still want to be with me after this then they are keepers!
- **Find people in like-minded places:** If you enjoy gaming, meet people at games shops. If you like plane spotting, get talking to those who do too. I think this is the best way to find 'your people'.
- **Meet online friends face to face:** The leap from online to face to face can feel a little scary but many of the parents and carers I spoke to commented on how relatively easy the transition was, as their online conversations meant that when they met in real life for the first time, they could jump straight into interesting conversations: 'Some of the best people in my support network are the best because we can have lovely neurodivergent in-depth conversations without the need for boring small talk before.'
- **Be yourself:** Just be yourself. Don't bend or change who you are for anyone. You are you! Be true to yourself. If you want to dye your hair rainbow colours, go do it. Find your tribe that understands and celebrates you. If people like you, they're the good ones, you don't need people who don't get you in your life.
- **Join parent–child groups:** I have found making friends so hard all my adult life and often feel lonely and isolated. I don't enjoy things like parties or social events, and I don't join groups on the whole. However, joining playgroups when my daughter was a baby was a massive help as I did find some like-minded people to hang around with at the park or meet for a coffee. It made the days easier.

- **Find friends via hobbies:** I have a wide circle of 'friends', or perhaps more acquaintances, through my hobbies. I regularly sing in choirs and I'm a bellringer too. Both of these activities involve lots of people and can be done all over so it gives me an immediate group to identify with if I move. Having a dog also helps as walkers get to know each other.
- **Have a range of different friends:** I think it's important to recognize there are different friends for different things. Not all are deep friendships.
- **Be open to opportunity:** Friends come unexpectedly and in the strangest of places and times. Stay open and connected and don't shut yourself down because of not having time or being too busy. You may find the best friend you'll ever have if you're brave enough to open yourself to opportunities. Protect your heart but be open in communication and be curious about what people have to say.
- **Seek out other neurodivergent adults:** Once your 'neurodar' is working efficiently, you will recognize other neurodiverse adults and children easily. Just remember they may not be as comfortable in their neurodivergence as you.
- **Let go of toxic friendships:** It's important to recognize not only those who make you feel comfortable, but also those who are toxic to you. For me, these people immediately make me feel like I'm back at school, trying to fit in. When I recognize that is happening, I can relax and stop trying, let the moment pass and move on.
- **No pressure:** Don't pressure yourself into needing friends. Don't try too hard. Give space.
- **Find balanced friendship:** It has taken me years to learn not to get sucked into the cycle of giving too much in my friendships. I'm a people pleaser and I always want to do the right thing, but sometimes it means I end up feeling used and taken for granted. I look at past friendships and realize

> they were really one-sided with me doing all the giving and the other person doing all the taking. Friendship shouldn't be like that. I guess what I'm saying is we need to be alive to this as a possibility and seek friendships where there is more balance, because this is a trap a lot of us can fall into.

As we conclude this chapter on making friends, it's evident that friendship can be a powerful source of support and connection in the lives of neurodivergent parents. Friendships can offer solace, understanding and moments of respite from the demands of parenting.

Whether you're someone who thrives on a large circle of friends or prefers a few deep connections, the tips shared by the community provide valuable insights into building and nurturing friendships. Take a moment to reflect on the role of friendship in your life, the challenges you've faced in balancing them with parenting, and the importance of being upfront and true to yourself in your social connections. Remember, the right friendships can be a source of strength, healing and joy on your journey.

YOUR TURN

Now, let's take a moment to reflect on the significance of friendship in your life, especially as a neurodivergent parent or caregiver. Consider the role it plays in your day-to-day engagement and enjoyment, the challenges you've faced in balancing friendships with parenting, and the importance of being upfront and true to yourself in your social connections.

Reflect on the importance of friendship in your life. How have friends made a difference in your day-to-day engagement with and enjoyment of life, especially as a neurodivergent parent or caregiver?

....

....

Consider the challenges of making and maintaining friends, particularly when facing the demands of parenting. Have you ever felt that you had limited time for friends due to the complexities of parenting? How did you manage this balance, and what impact did it have on your wellbeing?

Reflect on the idea of being upfront about your needs and limitations in friendships. Have you ever been open with friends about your preferences, such as your comfort level in social situations or the amount of time you can commit to socializing? How did this honesty affect your friendships?

Explore the concept of finding like-minded people in places related to your interests. Have you successfully made friends by engaging with others who share your hobbies or passions? Share your experiences of connecting with 'your people'.

Think about the importance of being yourself in friendships. Have you ever felt the need to change or adapt your personality to fit in with a particular group of friends? How has embracing your true self and finding a tribe that celebrates you positively impacted your social connections?

....

....

....

....

CHAPTER 6

In-Depth: Using Your Neurodivergent Strengths in Your Parenting

In this chapter, we're going to focus on some of the strengths of neurodivergent parents/carers because we're pretty brilliant actually, and our families are lucky to have us. For the next few pages, we're going to focus on some of the common strengths within our community and some suggestions for how we can lean into these strengths so they can help us parent in a way that feels authentic to us and is of benefit to our families too.

The Ideas

For each theme in this book, we explore a range of ideas that you can adapt for use in your day-to-day life. These ideas are all inspired by fellow neurodivergent parents and carers who've shared what works for them.

The ideas explored in the following pages are:

- **Idea 1: Embrace Your Authenticity and Openness**
- **Idea 2: Lean into Your Determination and Resilience**
- **Idea 3: Advocate with Empathy**
- **Idea 4: Create a Safe, Predictable World**
- **Idea 5: Dive Deep and Hyper-Focus**

Idea 1: Embrace Your Authenticity and Openness

'Honest to a fault' is a way in which many of us might describe ourselves. Many of us speak an unfiltered truth and find it difficult to live a life that is anything other than true to our values. Whilst these traits could be viewed through a negative lens as challenges to be overcome, there are great benefits to a more honest, authentic and open way of living too.

Everyone knows where they stand with us; we can be relied upon not to shy away from the topics that others might find taboo and we can get very creative at finding ways of overcoming the obstacles that stand in the way of us living a life true to our values.

Shared Experiences: Things We Get Right

Before we dive into practical ideas about how to use your strengths in your parenting, I wanted first to share some of the experiences from our community.

> **'My blunt honesty has led to a super open, honest, authentic relationship with my daughters (sometimes I feel they should tell me less).'**

> **'I take time to talk things through with my boys, helping them understand their feelings and why they behaved in a certain way so that we can anticipate those triggers in future and avoid more problems. I also help them understand their feelings and how their bodies respond to anxiety/stress/overwhelm, for example – it gives them the tools to manage themselves a bit more going forward.'**

> **'Honesty is a big one and no topic is ever off the table so if my son ever asks me a question, he will get an honest answer. So far we have spoken about death, sex, periods and all manner of other things some of my neurotypical friends would never consider discussing with their children.'**

Three Things You Could Try

1. **Identify and embrace your personal values:** What are the things that really matter to you more than anything else and

inform every decision you make? If you've never stopped to consider this before, it's a helpful exercise to spend a few minutes doing so help you find your identity both as an individual and as a parent.

PERSONAL VALUES

The whole point of personal values is that they should be personal to you. But to get you thinking, here are some potential personal values to explore. Perhaps one or two of these words stand out to you or will help you discover your own right words.

- Kindness
- Honesty
- Integrity
- Loyalty
- Respect
- Courage
- Gratitude
- Generosity
- Compassion
- Success
- Justice
- Forgiveness
- Faith
- Humour
- Acceptance
- Joy
- Calmness
- Influence
- Bravery
- Selflessness
- Sustainability
- Dependability

Identifying what really matters to you and giving yourself permission to live a life that is aligned with these values can lead to small changes that make a huge difference to how life feels. When we start to live a life we're proud to live, we're also acting as great role models to our children who will, in turn, need to work out what their personal values are and, hopefully, live a life that embraces them.

2. **Tackle the tough stuff:** When faced with the kind of questions that might have many neurotypical adults running a mile, many of us simply answer the question in a really straightforward way. This is great news for our kids, who have a LOT of questions about stuff that many adults seem reluctant to discuss, and asking questions of an adult they trust is a safe way for them to learn.

   Topics I've found myself answering questions on over the years include body parts and bodily functions, periods, vaping, sexual activity and pleasure, rape, gender, bullying, panic attacks, why adults don't say what they mean, pubic hair and changing bodies, disability, abuse, homophobia, war and religion, to name but a few. I'm sure you'll have many of your own to add to the list too.

   The thing is, when your child asks you a question like 'What is a clitoris?' they want to know and they tend to appreciate a straightforward answer. For me and perhaps for you too, that's easy, but for our neurotypical friends, this kind of question tends to leave them tongue-tied. That's okay, but don't assume that their silence or embarrassment is a model the rest of us have to follow. We can do it our way and our kids are likely to benefit greatly from having their questions answered and having a safe space to ask questions rather than relying on third-hand playground myths or unfiltered Google responses.

   So, if you notice that other people parent differently in this regard, don't change, keep it real and keep tackling the tough stuff; it might not be typical, but your children will benefit.

However, it's crucial to remember that not all children are emotionally ready for the same level of information. Each child is unique, and it's essential to gauge their emotional readiness when addressing sensitive topics. What might be appropriate for one child might not be for another. So, whilst I believe we should be addressing their questions honestly, we should also consider the emotional readiness of our children, ensuring that they receive information that they can understand and handle at their own pace.

3. **Say the good stuff out loud:** Some of us might gain a reputation for telling the truth even when, perhaps, people didn't want to hear it. This is because people ask questions sometimes when what they really want is reassurance... They ask, 'Does my bum look big in this?' and the correct response is some sort of fawning over how lovely they look even if they don't look lovely or you don't care. Inadvertently upsetting people in this kind of way can mean that over time we are more likely to keep our opinions to ourselves; but whilst that can prevent us from upsetting people, it can also prevent us for bringing them joy too. Sometimes the thoughts in our head are about how brilliant or beautiful someone is. If you're someone who has the urge to tell people the good stuff, do it!

   Spontaneous, sincere, specific compliments feel fantastic to receive and can be a real self-esteem boost for our children. Imagine how good it feels as a kid to hear an adult you love and trust take time to really notice your behaviour and say something like 'I loved how you patiently helped your brother eat his breakfast. It can be quite tricky encouraging him to eat but he gobbled up his Weetabix because you spoke to him kindly and made it fun for him too.'

   Our children observing us picking up on the positives in the people and places around us can also help them to view the world through a more positive lens too, so don't shy away, say the good stuff out loud.

Reflection

What's working well? What are you already doing? Could you do more of it?

....

....

....

....

What would you like to change?

....

....

....

....

What new ideas could you try?

....

....

....

....

My next tiny step is... What tiny step could you commit to taking today or tomorrow to work towards a different way of doing things?

....

....

....

....

Notes

....

....

....

....

Idea 2: Lean into Your Determination and Resilience

'Tenacious', 'resilient' and 'determined' were words that came up repeatedly when I asked neurodivergent adults to list their strengths. When something matters to us we seem to be able to go to superhuman lengths to make it happen, often focusing solely on the issue until it's resolved in a way that seems impossible to our neurotypical peers. This can be a real asset to our families and our kids if we can learn to harness it and perhaps bring other people along for the ride too.

Shared Experiences: Things We Get Right

Before we dive into practical ideas about how to use your strengths in your parenting, I wanted first to share some of the experiences from our community.

> **'Every one of my children have told me that they are glad I'm their mum. They feel free to crumble when life gets too overwhelming and are able to ask for help because they know I'll catch them, dust them down, set them back on their feet and never judge them. They know I know how their brain ticks.'**

> **'Once I have a mission, I'm not going to deviate from it until it's done. Most of my missions centre around my kids and their needs.'**

> **'I tend to see things from a different perspective than others, so when my son is struggling to access something due to his special needs, I can almost always see another way. I'll just keep coming up with ideas and trying them out until we've found a way to make it work.'**

Three Things You Could Try

1. **Set your own agenda – if it matters to you, pursue it:** Many of us have a deep sense of justice and fairness that can drive

our thoughts and actions. Whilst other people might be able to move on from something that's not right, our thoughts often get stuck there. That's not necessarily a bad thing; often the things that matter to us are things that really, really matter. It's just that other people have sometimes learned that it's hard to make things change and so they move onto the next worry whilst we're still grappling with massive problems like the climate crisis, a lack of reasonable adjustments for our child or institutional racism.

Change is hard, but we can be very determined and things will never change if there aren't people like us who are keen to champion important causes. So if it matters to you, it matters. Don't be afraid to keep fighting for what you believe in. Sometimes this will be of direct benefit to your children because you'll be fighting for causes related to them. Other times it will benefit them indirectly because you're trying to make the world a better place and also because they'll have one hell of a role model to learn from.

2. **Bring others on the journey too:** Our determination and tunnel vision can leave us a little isolated in our endeavours sometimes. It can also lead to burnout if left unchecked as we can be so focused on our goal that we become neglectful of self-care. One way to mitigate this is to find some allies amongst our family and friends. Whilst others are likely to lack the laser focus we have, there may be people who are interested and keen to help along the way or who we can ask to notice when we might be flagging (we might not notice ourselves) and might need some help to carry our load.

   A friend of mine exemplified this beautifully recently when they went on a one-woman mission to raise money for a cancer charity following the death of a loved one. Whilst I was in awe of the work she was doing, I was worried about her wellbeing so I asked how others could help. At first, she was reluctant to step back and invite others in, but after a little reflection, she came up with a list of jobs for an upcoming event she was organizing. From her friends, all stood in the sidelines and keen to help, she recruited bakers, sign makers and money takers. The event ended up far bigger and better than she could have managed alone and her friends were pleased to step up for her. So, when embarking on your latest mission, consider whether it needs to be a solo one or whether there might be some willing co-pilots. Don't expect them to commit to the issue as thoroughly as you do, but that doesn't mean they don't have an important part to play.

3. **Learn your times to shine and be shiny:** There might be a lot of situations in which you feel a bit like a fish out of water, but I'll bet there are others when those around you are struggling and you seem to find it relatively easy? For example, many neurodivergent adults report that, like me, day-to-day life can feel very challenging and provoke a great deal of anxiety, but when faced with a genuine crisis they are brilliant. Similarly, I have no fear of public speaking and am most comfortable on stage in front of hundreds of people, whilst I find one-to-one and small group conversations incredibly challenging. Notice the moments in life when you seem to be more resilient than those around you and step up when you find yourself in these situations.

Reflection

What's working well? What are you already doing? Could you do more of it?

....

....

....

....

What would you like to change?

....

....

....

....

What new ideas could you try?

....

....

....

....

My next tiny step is... What tiny step could you commit to taking today or tomorrow to work towards a different way of doing things?

....

....

....

....

Notes

....

....

....

....

Idea 3: Advocate with Empathy

Another strength many neurodivergent parents and carers highlighted was their ability to be brilliant advocates for their children. We will often fight longer, harder and with more insight than anyone else ever could or would. This is great news for our children, so let's explore some ways to channel that energy positively.

Shared Experiences: Things We Get Right

Before we dive into practical ideas about how to use your strengths in your parenting, I wanted first to share some of the experiences from our community.

> **'I see my daughter as an individual and recognize and meet her needs.'**

> **'The thing I get really right is our awareness and understanding of our neurodivergence. My children know their needs and are amazing advocates for both themselves and others.'**

> **'I am good at not pushing my kids to do things just because "that's what you do". I try to look at the big long-term goals (independence, confidence, self-esteem, kindness) and think about whether "the expected thing" is actually serving that goal, or whether we can move towards that goal better for us via another route. Some things that "everyone does" just don't need doing at all. I think that actually helps my kids to try new things because I can explain a proper reason/endpoint that they value, not just "because I said so" or "it's what all the other kids are doing so you should do it too".'**

> **'I have learnt that my job is to provide opportunities for my girls and accepting that it is up to them what they do with them. For example, we go to the zoo, but the car journey there is by far the best bit of the day. The zoo bit is filled with anxiety, strops (mostly mine), moaning and the occasional animal. But that's okay. Win some, lose some. I did my bit, and I've learnt what might work better next time. I like not having expectations (most of the time, I don't catch them all) on what family time should be like any more. Much more fun to live life without that pressure.'**

Three Things You Could Try

1. **Seek allies who recognize the importance of your point of view:** Many of us will have children who are autistic, ADHD, dyspraxic, dyslexic or some other flavour of neurospicy. Unlike neurotypical adults, we have a window directly into their world experience, which can mean we fight harder for them and can offer suggestions that are likely to be effective. We may not be experts in the field, but we are an expert in our child and in what it feels like to be a neurodivergent person trying to manage in a neurotypical world.

   Our point of view really matters and needs to be heard. When acting as a champion for your child, seek allies who acknowledge the importance of your voice and your experience. This might not be the most senior person in the room, but they will be the one who is most able to make things feel different for your child. So, if you feel unheard by the head teacher but there's a teaching assistant who gets it, gravitate towards them. You'll make a strong team and you'll make far better progress working alongside a more junior member of staff who's pulling with you than with a more senior member of staff who's pushing you away.

2. **Say the quiet part out loud:** 'You always say the quiet part out loud' was a compliment paid to one of the neurodivergent parents who contributed to this book when she asked her family what they thought her strengths were. I love this beautiful phrase and think it's something we can all embrace.

   Sometimes our children need someone there to say the quiet part out loud for them. They need an advocate who tells the truth and doesn't let the seemingly small stuff get forgotten. They need someone who will not shy away from difficult conversations and who can comprehend and communicate their point of view effectively so that others can begin to understand.

   For example, one carer told me about how her foster son's teacher contacted her to talk about his lack of focus and attention in class. Instead of agreeing with the teacher, she quietly challenged the narrative by talking about her foster son's ability to hyper-focus on subjects that he was keenly interested in. She told the teacher that she was confident that anything related to big cats would provide a way in to seeing a very different side of him and that this could be an important step in allowing him to feel some success in class rather than a constant feeling of failing when he was picked up for failing to focus.

This was a turning point for her foster son, whose strengths had gone unrecognized in the past and who responded well to the positive feedback he received when he did a beautiful project about jaguars. He started to do a little better at school and the relationship between him and his foster mum also went from strength to strength.

By empathetically communicating the parts of our child's story that could so easily be forgotten but that really matter, we give them a story they can begin to tell themselves in time and, every step along the way, we help them realize that they are never alone. There will always be someone alongside them who understands them and loves them enough to fight for them.

3. **Offer creative solutions:** Getting by as a neurodivergent person in a neurotypical world means that we have often become very creative in our approach to problem-solving. Life throws challenges at us all day, every day, and somehow we're still standing. This means we have a lifetime's worth of ideas to draw on and also a brain that is brilliant at finding novel ways through things. It can be easy to take these skills and experiences for granted or even to dismiss them. We draw on them so frequently that they feel normal, and we probably aren't managing perfectly all the time, which can make us focus on the moments it goes wrong.

   Take a step back and start to try and notice the creative solutions you come up with every day, for yourself and for your children. In the last 24 hours, examples from myself and my own daughters would include:

- putting sunglasses on in a too-bright shop
- creating a fidget toy out of a crisp packet when we had none of the right things to hand in a nervous energy moment
- asking for seats right at the front of the cinema to overcome some of the feelings of social anxiety from being around a lot of people (because everyone was behind us we felt less aware of all the people)
- skipping and jumping home as a fun way to dissipate anxious energy
- thrusting a dog into my daughter's arms and telling her it needed a cuddle at a point when I could see she was beginning to show signs of overwhelm.

Try to move away from taking these little moments of problem-solving for granted and realize that whilst they may not all succeed, your ideas are well worth exploring. When advocating for your child, share these ideas and look to encourage more creative problem-solving from your child and from other adults involved in their care.

Reflection

What's working well? What are you already doing? Could you do more of it?

....

....

....

....

What would you like to change?

....

....

....

....

What new ideas could you try?

....

....

....

....

My next tiny step is... What tiny step could you commit to taking today or tomorrow to work towards a different way of doing things?

....

....

....

....

Notes

....

....

....

....

Idea 4: Create a Safe Predictable World

Something that many of us have in common is our keenness and ability to try and create calm out of chaos and bring some sort of order to the world. Because the world can feel so unpredictable and baffling to us, bringing some sort of control and order gives us at least some things that we can rely on and predict. This sense of calm and control can help us better manage to navigate the day-to-day and gives us more bandwidth for being the best parent we're able to be. I find calm through my colour-ordered books, through morning and evening routines and through the rituals that I go through when going to new places. You may well have your own things which are a part of your everyday day which help you to feel a little more at peace with the crazy world in which we find ourselves living.

The good news is that in creating a world that feels safe, calm and predictable for us, we're creating a fantastic environment for our children too. Whilst children are finding their way in the world, it feels just as scary and unpredictable to them as it can to us. This is true even if they're neurotypical, as so many things are still new to them. Safe, calm, predictable environments are places where children can become bolder and braver and really begin to thrive. So, you might choose to embrace some of the things you do to control your world, happy in the knowledge that you're helping not just yourself but your children too.

Acknowledging Flexibility in Routines and Rituals

However, it's important to recognize that children can sometimes disrupt our routines and rituals. Parenting can be unpredictable, and children may have their own needs and challenges, causing our routines to go off track. This can be particularly challenging for neurodivergent parents, who may rely on routines to manage and navigate their daily lives.

It's crucial, especially for new parents or those about to become parents, to acknowledge that routines and rituals need flexibility as children are highly unpredictable. Whilst we strive for order and predictability, we must also be prepared for the unexpected and be adaptable when disruptions occur. This flexibility is a valuable but challenging skill in parenting, and we won't always succeed.

Shared Experiences: Things We Get Right

Before we dive into practical ideas about how to use your strengths in your parenting, I wanted first to share some of the experiences from our community.

'I am organized, with great routines and complete consistency.'

'Our home is their safe space – we all coexist really peacefully here – and everyone has their own "zones" that no one else gets to disturb them in when they need that space. It's our sanctuary.'

'I am consistent. Once I make a parenting plan I always see it through.'

'My strength is my understanding that just one word in a sentence or instruction is a whole unit of information that needs explaining and unpicking before my son can understand it. I think I get this really right because I get what it's like wondering what something/someone really means.'

'I love our low-arousal lifestyle.'

'One thing I think I really get right is not reacting right away to every little outburst. I understand that my daughter needs time to process, and she may yell and get angry for a moment, but if I remain calm whilst she processes then she will usually calm down and reach understanding within a minute or two, but if I react to her verbal outbursts it will quickly turn into a meltdown.'

Three Things You Could Try

1. **Routines:** Doing things the same way over and over again can make even the most challenging tasks begin to feel more safe and familiar. Routines can be inserted into almost any part of the day and after a while we can begin to do things almost on autopilot, which can free up a lot of mental energy and make us less likely to forget things. My teenage daughters are often keen to develop routines for themselves too and love watching other people's morning/evening/study and similar routines on YouTube.

As a society, we're often very good about things like bedtime routines with little children but this tends to drop off over time. Adolescents and adults can benefit from routines too, so long as the routine is developed together and feels like a good fit for everyone who'll be using it.

We love a routine in our house. Our current evening routine is:

- dinner
- shower
- devices away
- watch an episode of a TV show together
- solo wind-down time (I journal, do a little yoga and read)
- bedtime.

We're not perfect so it falls by the wayside sometimes, but having a routine really helps all of us to wind down and sleep better, and tweaking or re-establishing the evening routine is often our first port of call if any of us is feeling tired or at risk of burnout.

2. **Rules:** Rules are another way to make the world feel predictable and many of us have all sorts of rules for ourselves. If you're a black-and-white thinker, you may find you naturally gravitate towards rules. These can be beneficial to your children too because rules mean that our children know exactly what to expect of us and what we expect of them.

   Having a few simple rules is generally very effective; you need few enough that they can easily be remembered, so when using them as part of your parenting, think about what matters most right now. I've also found that the most effective rules are those that are decided as a family and that everyone is motivated by. For example, we have a rule about no phones at mealtimes. This is a rule my children suggested when they were little, before they had phones, because they didn't think their dad and I should use screens at the table. Now they have their own devices they adhere to the same rules and we all have better mealtimes as a result. It only works because everyone in our family is motivated by this rule, which makes it easy to follow.

3. **Rituals:** Like routines, rituals can make hard things feel easier by bringing a feeling of familiarity to a potentially challenging situation. You may have all sorts of rituals that might seem strange to other people but which bring a sense of calm or joy to you. I have a favourite teaspoon that I always eat my breakfast with. It feels good, I like it, and as someone with a history of anorexia anything that feels good and safe around mealtimes is a plus.

   Think about what rituals you have that can make you feel safe and happy even in more challenging situations and then consider how you can use these kinds of rituals in your parenting too. Maybe you can develop rituals around saying goodnight or goodbye or tidying up or eating. There are endless possibilities. Rituals are brilliant for making you and your child feel safe and on familiar ground, and also for building a bridge between the two of you as the ritual will connect and bond you.

Reflection

What's working well? What are you already doing? Could you do more of it?

....

....

....

....

What would you like to change?

....

....

....

....

What new ideas could you try?

....

....

....

....

My next tiny step is... What tiny step could you commit to taking today or tomorrow to work towards a different way of doing things?

....

....

....

....

Notes

....

....

....

....

Idea 5: Dive Deep and Hyper-Focus

When it comes to focus, many of us are a little yin and yang. Sometimes we have a real challenge focusing, with our attention often flitting to the next thing. Other times, we are a study in focus with an ability to dive deep into a topic for hours and hours, zoning in to the point where the rest of the world simply fades away. This ability to hyper-focus sets us apart from our neurotypical peers and can be cultivated as another strength that works well for us both as an individual and in a caring capacity.

Shared Experiences: Things We Get Right

Before we dive into practical ideas about how to use your strengths in your parenting, I wanted first to share some of the experiences from our community.

> **'I think I play differently to other parents. As long as my boys and I are playing in a world where I understand the characters and the rules, then I'm right in there, part of that world and playing alongside them rather than just watching on like most parents seem to.'**
>
> **'We game for hours. It's an escape for both of us and a time when we deeply connect.'**
>
> **'I'm The Best at research. If my daughter wants to find out about a new hobby or learn to look after a new pet, I'm right in there, researching for hours so we both know exactly what we're letting ourselves in for!'**

Three Things You Could Try

1. **Invite your children to invite you into their world:** In addition to our personal deep interests, we can learn to adapt our hyper-focus to join our children in their world. If our children have hobbies, passions or interests of their own, whether it's gaming, animals or their favourite YouTube channel, asking them to induct us into their world and bringing even a fraction of our ability to hyper-focus can mean our children suddenly have an ally in their world. Additionally, it can be a whole lot of fun putting ourselves in the role of learner and watching our children shine.

   The challenge here is that hyper-focus isn't a thing many of us can just switch on. We generally need to be motivated, interested and in the right kind of environment. The environment we can control, the motivation may well come with the love of our children, but the interest may be harder to find if our children's interests and ours differ massively. My advice here would be, just for a few minutes, act 'as if'... Suspend your lack of interest in your child's interest (much as you would suspend your disbelief when engaging with a fantasy world in a book, film or game). Often, if your child is very passionate, whilst you act 'as if' interested, their interest can become infectious and you find yourself drawn into their world.

Being invited into your child's world, even for short periods, can be a great way to connect and bond and can feel especially rewarding if your child has deep interests that are not shared with others or valued by their peer group or wider society.

2. **Don't be shy about diving deep:** If you're blessed with the determination and ability to dive deep into new topics that inspire or interest you, go with it. This might set you apart from your neurotypical peers, who may be more into going with the flow and less into detailed research. Many of us will have had negative experiences in the past such as being labelled a 'geek' or 'weirdo' at school for our aptitude for research and learning. But we're not at school now and these skills have genuine value both in terms of bringing us joy or reassurance and in terms of our ability to contribute something special to any team or group we're part of. For example, several of the parents who shared their experience for this book talked about the hours of research they pour into holiday planning, which is of great benefit to their families.

   Try to recognize this gift for what it is and refocus on it through a positive lens. Yes, you might be unusual and different from the norm, but instead of trying to hide what comes naturally and attempt to blend in and be like everyone else, embrace your inner geek and let it shine!

3. **Find how you find your flow:** Flow is that special state when you're so focused on a task or activity that time just seems to melt away. Hours can pass, you might forget to eat or realize

it's got dark outside without you noticing. Flow can provide a brilliant respite from the world whilst we engage our whole mind and body in something that feels really good for a little while. This can be anything from diving deeply into work or research to entering a different world through reading or gaming or finding ourselves completely consumed practising a skill or hobby.

The state of flow will happen naturally sometimes, but learning to voluntarily go there can be a great addition to our self-care toolbox, as a flow state is often one where we'll be able to reset and find a sense of emotional and sensory equilibrium. This is because whilst in flow, our worldview narrows and we spend some time in our own little world that feels good and safe.

The first step to being able to encourage a state of flow is to notice when it naturally happens. What kind of activities tend to draw you in and when and where has it happened? Looking to replicate the activity type and environmental factors can make a big difference. For me, it's knowing that the world is sleeping and there are no pressures on my time. This book was almost entirely written between the hours of 4 a.m. and 7 a.m., which is my special time when the world is quiet, my family are sleeping and I can dive deep into a flow state and get superhuman amounts of work done and feel great about it too.

Other things that can help are to ring-fence time for deep focus and put our devices (and physical selves) on 'Do Not Disturb' for a little while. It is also a good idea to make sure we've got snacks and drinks to hand and that we've recently been to the toilet. If you're lucky enough to enter a deep state of flow, you may find you become totally unaware of your basic physical needs, so think about them upfront so you don't move suddenly from beautiful flow to dysregulated hell when your body's needs finally take over.

Reflection

What's working well? What are you already doing? Could you do more of it?

....

....

....

....

What would you like to change?

....

....

....

....

What new ideas could you try?

....

....

....

....

My next tiny step is... What tiny step could you commit to taking today or tomorrow to work towards a different way of doing things?

....

....

....

....

Notes

....

....

....

....

Summary

To wrap up, here's a quick reference summary of the ideas shared in this chapter.

Idea 1: Embrace Your Authenticity and Openness
Many neurodivergent individuals describe themselves as 'honest to a fault', valuing an unfiltered truth and a life aligned with their values. This authenticity and openness, often seen as challenging traits, offer significant advantages. Neurodivergent parents create honest, authentic and open relationships with their children, discussing topics others might consider taboo, and finding creative ways to overcome obstacles.

Idea 2: Lean into Your Determination and Resilience
Neurodivergent parents often exhibit remarkable determination and resilience, which can be harnessed as a valuable strength in parenting. When something deeply matters to us, we possess the tenacity to go to great lengths to resolve it, often with a single-minded focus that amazes others.

Idea 3: Advocate with Empathy
Neurodivergent parents are brilliant advocates for our children, fighting longer and harder with insightful understanding. We excel at recognizing and meeting our children's individual needs and prioritize long-term goals over societal expectations.

Idea 4: Create a Safe, Predictable World
Many neurodivergent parents seek to create calm out of chaos and bring order to their world to find peace and control. By doing so, we provide our children with safe, calm and predictable environments, allowing them to thrive.

Idea 5: Dive Deep and Hyper-Focus
Neurodivergent parents possess the unique ability to hyper-focus, delving deeply into their interests and tasks for extended periods. This capacity for intense concentration can be channelled into parenting as a valuable asset.

Section 2

NAVIGATING NEURODIVERSITY'S CHALLENGES

In this section, we delve into the challenges that neurodivergent parents often face. From sensory differences and handling unsupportive people to managing intense emotions like anger and anxiety, this section equips you with strategies to navigate these external and internal hurdles.

CHAPTER 7

Quick Read: Sensory Differences

We experience the world differently to our neurotypical peers and this can make day-to-day activities that others complete with ease feel incredibly challenging to us. The community had lots of ideas to share about how they manage their sensory needs alongside their caring roles. I hope some of these will work for you too.

- **Respect your own needs:** Respect your own needs and don't constantly push yourself out of your comfort zone. It's exhausting being a parent, and fighting your own sensory needs will exhaust you even more.
- **Get curious about your triggers:** Learn what is going on for you and what your triggers are. Avoid the things that don't feel good unless they're essential. Saying no to soft play is okay!
- **Seek what soothes:** Don't push through if you don't have to. Noise is a massive one for me so sitting in silence is a massive recharger. I think, 'how can I enable this to happen?' Sometimes I go for a walk in nature, or I might take the car instead of forcing myself to walk in the rain, or I'll blow dry my hair – one of my sensory soothers.
- **Make a safe space:** Create a little nook or space where you have a safe environment you can retreat to. Imagine yourself there if situations get overwhelming.
- **Make changes:** Being aware is vital. Make changes. Don't be afraid to buy a new fridge because the sound of the fan was driving you insane. If supermarkets overwhelm you shop online. If soft play is too much go to the park, even if it's

raining. Those seemingly insignificant changes to others will be huge to you and your wellbeing.

- **Create your own PPE:** I don't go anywhere without my 'PPE' – personal protective equipment – that enables me to manage a little better in a neurotypical world. My PPE has noise-cancelling headphones, scented putty, a pair of sunglasses and chewing gum but everyone will find different things helpful.
- **Find compromises that work:** I have had to learn over the years to allow physical touch. I do not like to be touched around the neck so I had to instruct my child to cuddle me under the arms or around the waist. Even now he is six foot tall he still goes under my arms rather than around the neck.
- **Make it work at work:** I'm autistic and ADHD and I love my job but the office is a challenging environment for me. Sometimes I'm sensory seeking; things that can help with this are my standing desk, walking meetings or running errands (I'm always the one making the tea or doing the photocopying). I also have a drawer full of fidgets and listen to death metal really loudly through my headphones if I'm craving noise.

  Other times, if I need calming, then I'll switch my music to classical, I'll step outside and watch the clouds or I'll go and spend a few minutes in the disabled toilet where I know I won't be disturbed. Talking to my boss and colleagues about my needs has really helped too. I used to feel guilty and like I was letting the team down, but now we talk more openly about it I've learnt that whilst I might do things a bit differently to everyone else, my contribution is valid and valued.
- **Your child's needs may differ from yours:** Although I struggle with some food textures I always made sure I allowed my child to try all textures and tastes, even those that I struggled with. He has less texture and taste issues than I do, luckily, and is not really that fussy with foods and will try most new foods.
- **Find what works for everyone:** Some activities might feel good for the whole family. This is great because as a parent, you

can't always remove yourself from your family life in order to meet your own needs right now. In our family, if it's been a heavy day, we find that heading to the sea for a few minutes really helps. We all have different needs but the sound of the sea, watching the waves, feeling the pebbles beneath our feet and breathing in the fresh sea air makes all of us feel better.

- **Make your family aware:** Explain your challenges to your family and how they can help you; if they have their own needs you can encourage them to do the same. In our house, the dinner table can be hell with seven people, six of whom are neurodivergent, so I explain if I'm overwhelmed.
- **Be aware of any potentially harmful issues:** Pain threshold is a big one. Explain this to health professionals so they can understand. You might not be processing the pain like others do, but it doesn't mean the issue isn't as serious. My son broke his leg recently but was not screaming in pain. In A&E he was dismissed and sent to the back of the queue as staff thought he would be screaming if he'd broken it. I had to be quite firm with nurses and in my conviction to get him an X-ray which, of course, proved our suspicions to be correct.

  Author's note: When I read the above story about a mum and her son's broken leg, I had a bit of an aha moment about the very start of my own parenting journey, back before I knew I was autistic. Like many parents, I went to NCT classes to learn about birth and early parenting. I remember being very worried that I wouldn't know when I was in labour as I have a pretty high pain threshold. My concerns were dismissed by the class leader and other mums I mentioned them to. I was generally met with a chuckle, an eye roll and something along the lines of 'Oh you'll know...'. So I assumed I would know. In short, I didn't. What I mistook for possible Braxton Hicks was full-blown labour and Lyra was rather unceremoniously born in our toilet when I thought I really needed a wee.

In this Quick Read, we've delved into the world of sensory differences and how they impact our lives as neurodivergent parents and caregivers. It's clear that navigating these sensory sensitivities can be both challenging and enlightening. The insights and strategies shared by our community shed light on the importance of self-respect, self-care and understanding our unique sensory triggers. As you reflect on your own sensory needs and experiences, remember that you're not alone on this journey. Your understanding of these differences and your commitment to managing them effectively can lead to a more balanced and fulfilling life as a neurodivergent individual and parent.

YOUR TURN

Now, let's take a moment to reflect on your own sensory needs and experiences. Are there specific triggers or sensitivities you've become aware of as a neurodivergent parent or caregiver? How have you managed these sensitivities, and what strategies can you use to enhance your overall wellbeing? You can explore these questions and more using the following prompts.

Reflect on your own sensory needs and experiences. Are there specific sensory triggers or sensitivities that you've become aware of as a neurodivergent parent or caregiver? What strategies can you use to manage these sensitivities?

....

....

....

....

Consider the importance of respecting your own sensory needs. Have you ever felt the pressure to push yourself out of your comfort zone, especially as a parent? How has this affected your wellbeing, and what steps have you taken to prioritize your sensory comfort?

....

....

Explore the concept of creating a safe space or retreat for yourself. Have you established a particular environment or space where you can seek comfort when sensory challenges become overwhelming? Describe this space and its significance in helping you cope.

Reflect on the idea of finding compromises, especially in physical touch. Have you encountered situations where physical touch is challenging for you but you've found ways to navigate them, such as instructing your child on how to hug you differently? Share any experiences or insights regarding sensory compromises.

Think about the importance of making your family aware of your sensory challenges. Have you communicated your sensory sensitivities to your family members, and how have they responded? Consider strategies for explaining your needs to your loved ones effectively.

CHAPTER 8

Quick Read: Unsupportive People

In our journey as neurodivergent adults, we often find ourselves facing unsupportive or unkind individuals who may not fully understand our unique perspectives and parenting approaches. Whilst diversity in thought and action is a natural part of the human experience, managing these challenging interactions is crucial to our overall wellbeing and our ability to parent effectively. It's certainly a path I've found myself needing to tread carefully, especially as my mental filters tend to mean I cling onto 'evidence' of my bad parenting and readily dismiss the good stuff. Over the years, I've come to accept that there is no one right way, and my way will always be the wrong way according to somebody. These days, I try to look to the evidence directly in front of me – my girls. If the way we parent and live makes life feel better for my girls and they're more able to thrive, then this is all the evidence that I need that it's the right thing to do.

With practice, I've become better at tuning out (or completely estranging myself from) the naysayers. But I'd be lying if I said it had been easy – there are still days when I'm full of self-doubt, loathing and fear. On those days, I chat to my good friends Ellie and Nerys who I know have my back. I know they will provide me reassurance but will also tell me honestly if I need to do something differently. Our little trio has helped me through many difficult days and is certainly a far better tonic than immersing myself in the poison of those who dislike me or disagree with my approach.

This quick-read chapter explores strategies for navigating unsupportive relationships with grace and resilience, drawing from the diverse experiences and wisdom of our community.

The contributors to this book have shared a wealth of

insights, even when their approaches have differed. Some have advocated for the power of education and polite confrontation, whilst others have chosen the path of detachment and self-care. By examining these varied responses, we can discover valuable tools for maintaining our sense of self and wellbeing, regardless of the unsupportive forces we encounter on our journey.

- **Speak out:** Be brave enough to speak out. It works for some people who feel they know everything and act like they're experts in something they know nothing about. They need to be politely educated or their ignorance politely spelt out to them. I'm polite but firm with strangers – 'Thank you for your concern. My child is struggling right now and this is their way of showing me.'
- **Understand when to move on:** I'm learning to identify when things are my responsibility and when they are not. That helps me understand when to be bothered about how someone reacts. I've spent a lot of my life worrying about upsetting people and trying to work out what I did to upset them, and now I'm trying to recognize when it's best to ignore and move on.
- **Thank you, next...** Simply say thank you, and make a note not to ask their advice later. Acknowledge they mean well, but may not have the skills or understanding to empathize with you.
- **Step into their shoes:** Ask yourself why you find them unsupportive and what they are doing that feels unsupportive. I think it is important to understand that each of us is different and have dealt with different people all our lives. That person may actually think they are being useful or supportive, as that is how they have been supportive to others (likely those who are not neurodivergent).
- **Don't expect mind reading:** With people you know, it is best to discuss this in an adult way as they will not know or

understand that what they are doing is not supportive unless you tell them! I have learned over the years that people are not mind readers and often I used to think things and believe that people should know what my thoughts were... but they don't. We need to tell them what we think they're doing wrong if we'd like it to change in the future.

- **Listen:** Listen with curiosity and without judgement (it's difficult but worth it). Once you understand more about where someone is coming from, this provides an opportunity to educate them in turn, which will not only benefit them as a parent and their child but potentially others as well.
- **Avoid:** If people don't enhance my life, I avoid them. Making intentional choices about our social interactions has been crucial for our family's wellbeing. I'm constantly evaluating the people in our lives and the impact they have on us. For example, there have been situations where we've found it necessary to minimize contact with certain friends because their children's comments or behaviour have caused discomfort and distress for my kids. We've also encountered instances where the caregiving methods of some friends seemed to encourage our children to mask their neurodivergent traits and comply with societal expectations. Whilst we respect diverse parenting approaches, it became important for us to prioritize our children's authenticity and wellbeing, so we chose to spend less time with those friends moving forwards.
- **Educate:** Explain, explain and explain again, with patience and living examples of positive experiences. I explained dysregulation through nail biting, pen tapping, their own special interests, stimming, or the coke bottle analogy, and often found that the adult said things like 'well, I do that and there's nothing wrong with me', which allowed me to finish with 'and there's nothing wrong with my child either'. Cue mic-drop...
- **Block/mute/delete:** If people are unsupportive or unpleasant online I don't hesitate to block or mute them. I'll report them

if appropriate. I also delete comments that I think are unkind or unhelpful. I am happy to receive constructive feedback, but some people are just mean and I can choose to either listen and let their sour remarks remain or delete them... I choose the latter.

- **Keep note of nice things:** For every person who criticizes you or is unsupportive, there are often many more who are kind, supportive or thankful. Keeping a file of the kind things that people say or do or the supportive comments you receive can give you something really nice to reflect on in the moments when an unsupportive interaction has really got you down. The negative stuff tends to loom large in our minds, so having a whole file of lovely things like thank you cards or memories about sweet things people have said or done can be a good way to drown out individual negative moments.

Our journey as neurodivergent adults and parents is undeniably unique, and we must navigate a world filled with diverse perspectives and attitudes. The insights shared in this chapter reflect the wisdom of a community that knows the value of grace and resilience when confronted with unsupportive individuals. Whether through polite education, self-care or choosing to move forward with a sense of self-preservation, we can discover that we possess the strength to thrive despite the unsupportive forces we may encounter. As we delve into the reflections ahead, consider the strategies offered here and embrace the power of your own journey, knowing that you are not alone in facing these challenges.

YOUR TURN

Now, let's take a moment to reflect on your own experiences with unsupportive or negative comments from others regarding your parenting or neurodivergent needs. How did you handle these situations, and what emotions did they evoke? Have you ever tried to educate or politely confront someone who misunderstood your neurodivergent needs or parenting approach? How did that go? What strategies have you developed to cope with or respond to these interactions? You can explore these questions and more using the following prompts.

Reflect on a time when you encountered unsupportive or negative comments from others about your parenting or neurodivergent needs. How did you handle the situation, and what emotions did it evoke? What strategies have you used to cope or respond to such interactions?

Consider the idea of speaking out and educating unsupportive individuals. Have you ever tried to politely educate someone who misunderstood your neurodivergent needs or parenting approach? Write about your experiences and the outcomes of these conversations, whether positive or challenging.

Reflect on the concept of moving on and not internalizing negative interactions. How have you learned to differentiate between situations where someone's reaction is your responsibility and when it's best to let go and move on?

Explore the idea of listening without judgement. Have you ever actively listened to someone who had unsupportive views or opinions about neurodiversity? How did this experience affect your perspective, and did it lead to any meaningful conversations or changes in understanding?

....

....

....

....

Think about the importance of keeping note of positive interactions. Reflect on the impact of focusing on the positive, and note any ideas for maintaining a positive outlook in the face of unsupportive people.

....

....

....

....

CHAPTER 9

In-Depth: Managing Meltdown and Shutdown

Meltdown and shutdown describe what happens when we become overwhelmed. This might be due to a number of different reasons, such as too much sensory or social input to process, or big demands being placed on our executive function (our ability to process, organize and plan). Whilst everyone's experience is a little different, it's common for overwhelm to result in either meltdown or shutdown for autistic/ADHD individuals.

- **Meltdown** is often big and noisy and might look like extreme anger or anxiety. It's when all of the overwhelm pours out of us in a big way.
- **Shutdown** looks very different and is when the overwhelm turns inwards. This can result in us freezing, dissociating or becoming distant. We might become mute or numb.

Overwhelm states such as meltdown and shutdown happen to adults as well as to children, which comes as a surprise to some people who think it's something that children grow out of, but as a woman in my forties who still experiences these states pretty often, I'm here to say that if this sounds like you, you're not alone.

> **'I'm a 53-year-old woman. I have spent years feeling like I should have grown out of this and I just assumed everyone else had even though I know autistic children grow into autistic adults.**
>
> **I've got tears streaming down my face as I write this because I was today years old when I realized that there are other people like me.**
>
> **I'm not the only one.**

I'm not a freak.

I'm not broken, just different.'

Entering meltdown or shutdown not only feels deeply distressing to us as individuals, it also makes it seriously difficult for us to carry out our parenting responsibilities, which is why I've dedicated the next few pages to exploring how we can avoid and manage these states. Meltdown and shutdown look very different, but the triggers and ways of managing them are largely similar so we'll address them together in this chapter.

Window of Tolerance

Before we jump in, I'm going to briefly explain the concept of the 'window of tolerance' – which is the therapeutic term for coping without becoming overwhelmed. It's a helpful concept to get your head around and can give you a simple way to explain things to your family too. The window of tolerance was originally devised by Dan Siegel. I'm sharing a very simplified model, adapted to help explain autistic meltdown and shutdown specifically (see Figure 9.1).

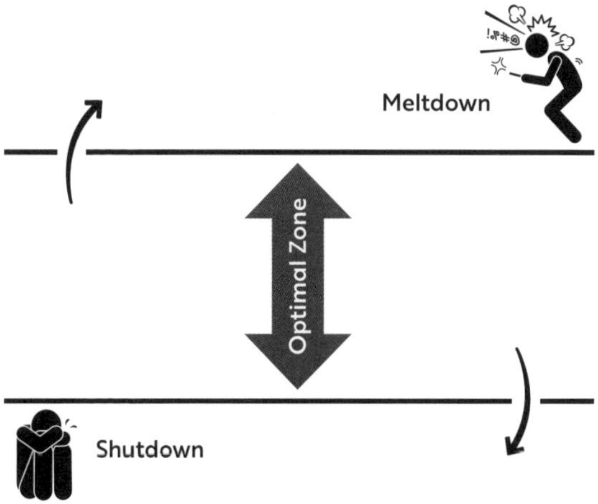

Figure 9.1 The window of tolerance: A visual representation of the optimal arousal zone where individuals can effectively manage and process stimuli and emotional experiences

When we are within our window of tolerance, we can cope with what's going on around us. We're able to engage, interact and sometimes enjoy the situation we find ourselves in.

Different inputs can affect where we sit within our window of tolerance; so loud noises or conversations might mean we're no longer sitting plumb in the middle of what we can tolerate, but we might still be safely within our window. We move around within it all the time. We become overwhelmed when we are no longer within our window of tolerance and we enter states of meltdown or shutdown.

A few things it's helpful to note about the window of tolerance:

- It's not an even playing field: some people have a naturally smaller window of tolerance. We're in that crew I'm afraid.
- You can take steps to increase your window of tolerance; sleep, diet, exercise and self-care can all contribute to a bigger window of tolerance and more ability to cope day to day.
- We can take proactive steps to keep ourselves within our window of tolerance, by helping ourselves to 'reset' and move more deeply within our optimal zone. Anything that calms or soothes us can help here.

It can be helpful to reflect on the things that push you towards and out of the edges of your window of tolerance, as well as thinking about the actions that help to keep you within it. This is an ongoing battle all day every day, and stopping simply to reflect on it can often help you realize the steps that you're perhaps unconsciously taking to enable you to cope each day. Becoming more aware of the things you're already doing can help you to consciously do those things more as well as consider what else you might add to your toolbox. There are lots of ideas within this chapter.

Shared Experiences: What Meltdown and Shutdown Feel Like

Meltdown and shutdown can feel different for different people and at different times. One of the hopes I had for this book was to normalize some of our experiences as neurodivergent parents and carers, and one of the ways I hoped to do that was to share a range of experiences so you could see that you're not alone in the day-to-day challenges you're facing and that there are a whole tribe of us that are also trying hard to manage.

When I asked parents and carers to share their experience of what meltdown and shutdown feels like for them, this is what they said:

> **'I can get very short-fused. I get very agitated and don't want to be spoken to or touched.'**

> **'I'm prone to self-harm, biting my hands or arms, pulling out my hair, hitting my head.'**

> **'I have extreme emotional outbursts so I'll start sobbing or shouting. I'm generally pretty chilled so this is a noticeable change.'**

> **'I've experienced physical shutdowns where my body has forced me to stop. These have been totally debilitating, leading to long recovery times. Other times, emotional overwhelm leads to extreme tiredness, like my body and brain are saying enough is enough and I need to recover.'**

> **'It usually starts with every single sound being too loud. Every texture too hard and spiky. I then develop an extreme inability to process new information and an inability to start new tasks no matter how urgent.'**

> **'I completely overreact to EVERYTHING. Left a cup on the drainer? You don't care about me at all. Didn't take your socks upstairs? You're deliberately trying to upset me.'**

'I completely lose it, flapping, can't breathe, walking around and around really fast back and forth, mind goes blank, can't think, can't listen or focus.'

'I swear, I mutter to myself, am verbally nasty to my partner and often walk or storm off.'

'Sometimes I hit my forehead with my hands. I foam at the mouth. My voice gets louder and I feel agitated and walk extremely quickly, like a strange energy has come over me.'

'I feel tearful and despairing. I have to retreat to be alone to avoid screaming, shouting or saying hurtful and unreasonable things to the people around me.'

'I lose my temper and scream and shout then cry afterwards that I've done it again and I'm such a terrible parent.'

'I stop responding, I just go into my shell and ignore everyone around me.'

'I feel very tense and experience a desire to escape. This may look like an anger outburst or that I appear very anxious. I will be restless and want to leave the situation.'

'Apparently I totally zone out. Like someone pulled the plug. It might take several attempts for someone to get my attention and then I'll respond as if I'm super sleepy or doped up.'

BALANCING FRAGILE LOADS: NAVIGATING OVERWHELM AND SELF-ACCEPTANCE

'It's like I am at the bottom of an escalator and there are boxes and packages full of crockery on every step and I have to catch them and place them gently down but they are coming too fast and they are too fragile and there are too many.

I have learnt not to presume that I am at fault. Catching

fragile boxes off escalators is not everyone's forté and I have plenty of other skills. But it feels like society says we should all be good at catching boxes, and occasionally modern society says it's okay not to be good at catching boxes, but they are not going to switch the escalator off or make the boxes less fragile or tell you not to bother catching the boxes.

So, I have to decide each time how much I care if I don't manage to catch the boxes. I sometimes ask for help catching the boxes and my friends and family tell me to go and sit on the sofa whilst they catch mine and their own boxes. This makes me feel guilty and useless.

Sometimes I swap escalators for one that is moving slower and isn't flashing lights at me. Or one without boxes full of chunky crockery. But the problem with this is that sometimes I am good at catching boxes and I really enjoy it when I can catch them faster and better than everyone else. Plus I like to feel included and useful.

As an adult, I am much better at recognizing when I am not coping before I am in meltdown mode. But occasionally I mistime it and start walking round in circles clutching my head and saying, I am overwhelmed. Then someone will sit me down and take over with my boxes until I feel better.'

Hopefully reading the experiences of others makes you feel a little less alone; that was certainly the overwhelming feeling that those of us working together on this book seemed to experience again and again: 'Oh, you too... I thought it was just me!'

You are not alone.

10 THINGS YOU NEED TO HEAR

Here are ten things that myself and other neurodivergent parents/carers thought it was important for you to hear:

1. You are not alone – we all pretend too much and we're all struggling behind closed doors.

2. Don't feel ashamed of your emotions – you aren't overreacting.
3. You aren't horrible or dramatic, you're just coping in the only way you know how.
4. High functioning isn't a thing. Some days we manage, some days we don't and we shouldn't be forced to pretend.
5. Creating a home environment that supports your sensory needs isn't selfish.
6. Overwhelm can make you angry and shouty. You're not a bad person, just an overwhelmed one.
7. Don't feel guilty for retreating – you'll be a better parent afterwards.
8. Many people want to help but need you to help them understand how.
9. Your kids love you more than you love yourself.
10. The tiniest things can lead to the biggest meltdowns.

The Ideas

For each theme in this book, we explore a range of ideas that you can adapt for use in your day-to-day life. These ideas are all inspired by fellow neurodivergent parents and carers who've shared what works for them.

The ideas explored in the following pages are:

- **Idea 1: Know, and Respect, Your Triggers**
- **Idea 2: Hunger Is the Enemy**
- **Idea 3: Just Say No**
- **Idea 4: Prepare Ahead**
- **Idea 5: Escape to a Solo Safe Space**
- **Idea 6: Find Family and Friends Who Get It**
- **Idea 7: Flip the Feeling with Your Special Interest**
- **Idea 8: Take Time to Reset and Regulate after Trigger Activities**

- **Idea 9: Have Shared Expectations about Communication**
- **Idea 10: Balance Your Boosters and Drainers**

Idea 1: Know, and Respect, Your Triggers

Getting to know what leads you to meltdown and shutdown can help reduce the frequency and severity of these situations. This means getting curious about the people, places, things and feelings that trigger a feeling of overwhelm for you.

Five Things You Could Try

1. **Journal and look for patterns:** Keeping a journal can help us to notice patterns in our behaviour and how well we're managing. Keeping a journal over days or weeks can help us start to see patterns. You could write long-form, but something as simple as rating how we're feeling on a scale of one to ten several times a day with a tiny bit of information about the context can help us quickly build a picture of what helps us and what hinders us.
2. **Rank potential triggers at times of calm:** Writing lists and ranking potential triggers can help you gain an understanding of what makes you struggle more. Always do this at a time of relative calm and happy as your overwhelmed brain will not be able to compute this kind of task well.
3. **Ask your family what they've noticed:** Those who know us well can often offer a lot of insight based on their observations on when, where and with whom we struggle. Sometimes, things can seem very obvious to them that we've never noticed about ourselves, so asking for their ideas and input can be very eye-opening. Ask them both about your triggers and also about the warning signs that things are about to get tricky.
4. **Use tricky times as a learning moment:** After you've experienced meltdown or shutdown and things are back on an

even keel, use it as an opportunity to learn a little bit more about yourself. Resist the urge to beat yourself up about what's happened and instead get really curious about what triggered the situation and what warning signs you might have missed this time but could look out for in future.

5. **Isolate triggers by experimenting:** Every situation is so complex that it can be hard to isolate what might have triggered us: was it the place, a person, something that happened? If you're not sure, consider all the potential things that could be triggering and then explore how you manage each of those things in a different context – for example, if you think a certain person is a trigger for you, explore whether they are still an issue if you spend time with them in a different context.

Reflection

What's working well? What are you already doing? Could you do more of it?

....

....

....

....

What would you like to change?

....

....

....

....

What new ideas could you try?

....

....

....

....

My next tiny step is... What tiny step could you commit to taking today or tomorrow to work towards a different way of doing things?

....

....

....

....

Notes

....

....

....

....

Idea 2: Hunger Is the Enemy

Meeting our basic physical needs is the cornerstone of maintaining emotional regulation, a crucial aspect of being the parent our children need. For many of us, hunger is not just an empty stomach; it's a pathway to emotional dysregulation, making it nearly impossible to be the composed, responsive adults our children depend on.

For many of us being hungry is the quickest route to meltdown and is a sure-fire way of making everything feel ten times harder to manage and sending our executive function through the window. The challenge here is that this can result in us forgetting to feed our children, or ourselves, which will, in turn, exacerbate the situation.

Here are some ideas to try to prevent this.

Five Things You Could Try

1. **Learn hunger cues:** One of the things many of us struggle with is recognizing when we're hungry, which can mean we

go to the point of hungry and beyond before we realize that we've got a basic physical need punching us in the gut.

Trying to learn a bit more about the physical and emotional signs that indicate that you might benefit from a snack can help prevent things from completely falling apart. This might mean tuning into a rumbling or empty stomach, noting that we're feeling a little light-headed or woozy, or picking up on changes in mood such as irritability or feeling low, which can be fuelled by hunger.

Other people might know your cues better than you, so it's worth asking your family. If you're really struggling with it, checking in with your body and mood just before mealtimes for a few days might help you notice some patterns.

2. **Develop a regular routine for meals and snacks:** Making sure that we eat regularly can be a good way of preventing us reaching the point where hunger becomes an issue. Additionally, eating at regular times can help your body get into a good rhythm.

   A pattern of smaller meals and snacks can help prevent big peaks and troughs of energy and lows for both us and our family (who'll benefit from regular meal and snack times too). This type of routine around meal and snack times can also speak to the need many of us have for order and consistency, so it has multiple benefits if we're able to make it work.

3. **Carry snacks with you for a quick boost:** Identifying some snacks that are portable and non-perishable such as nuts or cereal bars can mean that you always have something to hand when you're out and about if you feel hunger creeping up on you. I have various bars and snacks languishing in the bottom of bags and car boots, just in case... It's surprising how often they come in handy, especially if, like me, you're quite particular about what you are and are not happy to eat, which can make it trickier to buy a snack on the go.

   Fresh fruit and veg also makes a great snack and I'll often grab an apple on my way out of the house, but the joy of the non-perishable snacks is you can forget about them in the bottom of your bag and they're there when you need them, even on a day you weren't organized enough to grab a snack as you left home (my current go-to are dried apple rings as everyone in the family likes them and they bring a little sensory joy too).

4. **Eat first, finish the to-do list later:** Even once we get better at picking up our hunger cues it can be easy to choose to ignore them whilst we 'just finish x...' especially if we're in flow. But we ignore our hunger at our peril. Things can rapidly unravel if we start to get hungry, so if your watch or your body are telling you it's time for a snack, take a break and grab a snack. Carrying on for 'five more minutes' can easily turn into ten or thirty or three hours (just me?), so be kind to your body and your future self and grab a bite to eat.

5. **When out, think about where and when you'll eat:** One thing that can easily get in the way of us eating regular meals and snacks is being in different places. It's one thing to establish a pattern of meals and snacks at home or a regular workplace where we have more control of what food we can access and where we'll eat it. But especially when we're in less familiar places, this is trickier.

   Planning ahead and thinking about what your needs are in terms of food and places to eat it can make a big difference. Trying to source food and quiet spaces when you're already starting to run on a bit of an energy low can be a recipe for trouble.

   For me, this often looks like taking food with me and planning to head to my car for a few minutes. This is a plan I can ditch if I feel able to manage an alternative, but it means I know that I can and will eat. I also find it helpful to have a few ubiquitous chains that I know I'm happy to eat at too; for example, if I'm on the road and it's time to eat, I can often easily access a mozzarella and tomato panini from Costa, because you're never far from a Costa these days.

Reflection

What's working well? What are you already doing? Could you do more of it?

....

....

....

....

What would you like to change?

....

....

....

....

What new ideas could you try?

....

....

....

....

My next tiny step is... What tiny step could you commit to taking today or tomorrow to work towards a different way of doing things?

....

....

....

....

Notes

....

....

....

....

Idea 3: Just Say No

There are only so many hours in the day, so we need to think carefully about how we fill those hours. Even for our neurotypical pals this will mean a healthy dose of saying no to keep things in balance, but it's even more important for us where too many yeses can quickly lead to meltdown, shutdown or total burnout.

Five Things You Could Try

1. **Write a to-don't list:** I love a to-don't list. It can feel like a really powerful way of taking control. It's just as it sounds – a list of things we are NOT going to do. Good ways to generate your to-don't list can include:
   - **Considering the tasks we regularly do** and thinking honestly about whether they all need to be done, or whether they can either be stopped or done less frequently, or to a lower standard, buying ourselves a little extra time and energy.
   - **Things that other people want you to do for them** which have crept onto your to-do list but which should sit firmly on theirs. Your email inbox is a good place to hunt here for things to add to the 'nope' list – I regularly remind myself that my email inbox is 'other people's to-do lists' and try to prioritize my own to-do list first.
   - **Others may benefit from responsibility for some of your tasks.** It can be easy to hold onto tasks which could be beneficial to pass on. Our children will often benefit from learning how to do new tasks, such as making their own sandwich, packing a bag or ordering tickets for the film you want to see. At work, delegation can be a great way of growing the skills of team members who might respond well to leading on a small project or chairing a meeting. This can mean a little extra work initially whilst we teach our children or colleagues how to do new tasks, but it can be a worthwhile investment that permanently removes some items from our personal to-do list.

2. **Consider how you felt last time you were told no:** It can feel horrible to say no and we can end up tying ourselves in knots thinking about how awful we feel about it. We might assume that the person we're saying no to will think a whole bunch of horrible or irritated thoughts about us. The truth is, when we're the one doing the asking, a no is something that we generally bounce back from pretty quickly. It's worth just taking a mental note of any 'nos' you get in day-to-day life and how they make you feel and how quickly you move on to find an alternative. This understanding can make it a lot easier to say no next time the chance arises.

3. **Remember, 'No' is a complete sentence:** One of the benefits of being an adult is that you get to choose what you say yes to and no to. We don't owe anyone an explanation about why we're saying no. We may have all sorts of justifications for our decision, but 'No' really is a complete sentence and you're least likely to talk yourself out of your no if you keep it simple and firm.

4. **Think about what you're saying yes to when you say no:** When we say no to others, we say yes to ourselves. That sounds trite, but it's true. Think about exactly what you're saying yes to when you're strong enough to say no. I often remind myself when I'm turning down opportunities that I'm choosing to say yes to my family twice over. First, because the opportunity would have taken me away from them for the duration of the task and travel, and second, because I have to build in recovery time which may have been spent at home, but likely alone rather than with my loved ones.

   Increasingly, I also remind myself that when I say no to work, I say yes to fun – a mindset that my past therapist would rejoice in. If by turning down an unpaid work opportunity I give myself enough time that week to get out and paraglide then that is a positive choice in my book.

5. **Keep a record of things you said no to:** Learning to say no can take practice and can feel very hard at first. I honestly think

it's something you should take pride in and also role-model for your family too. Keeping a note of when you said no, what happened next or the reaction you got can build your confidence in saying no in future and help you to see that truly, nothing awful happens when you Just Say No.

Reflection

What's working well? What are you already doing? Could you do more of it?

....

....

....

....

What would you like to change?

....

....

....

....

What new ideas could you try?

....

....

....

....

My next tiny step is... What tiny step could you commit to taking today or tomorrow to work towards a different way of doing things?

....

....

....

....

Notes

....

....

....

....

Idea 4: Prepare Ahead

Using the times when we're managing well to plan and prepare ahead for other times that may get trickier can make a significant difference to our ability to manage well and parent well. This won't work for everyone, but even small amounts of pre-planning and preparing can make a big difference to our ability to cope day to day.

Five Things You Could Try

1. **Plan quiet times in advance for busier weeks:** Pre-plan your downtime, especially if the week ahead is looking busier than usual. Blocking the time you need to take out in your diary will make it much more possible and likely that you'll take the quiet time you need.

2. **Plan days out carefully in advance:** Days out can be a real challenge for us, but with careful planning it is possible for them to go well. Things that many of our neurotypical pals might breeze through can be trickier for us, so planning ahead is our friend.

PLANNING DAYS OUT

Things that it can be helpful to consider when planning days out include:

- **The journey:** How will you get there? Planning a walking, public transport or driving route ahead and being realistic about the amount of time needed can help.

- **Parking:** Remember to think about parking if you're driving. This is often a real trigger for me as when I arrive somewhere, I tend to think I can relax and then I'm faced with the new challenge of where on earth to leave my car, which can feel really challenging. Google Street View can help with sussing out potential parking options and issues at new places.
- **Food:** Think about what, when and where you'll eat.
- **The activity:** Having a good idea about what the day will entail and how long you hope to stay so you can manage your expectations and those of your family can help.
- **All the things:** What do you need to take with you? If you've got younger kids you may have a huge list of things you have to take everywhere (it gets better, I promise), and in addition to this you might need extra things: swimming stuff, shoes for specific activities, bread for the ducks... If you can, think ahead about what you might need so you're not caught out.
- **Safe spaces:** It can be helpful to know how you'll create a safe space for yourself if you need to regulate during the course of the day. This might be a place you can physically escape to, or it might be plugging yourself into some soothing music. Think about what is realistic and practical ahead of time as you won't be in a good place to figure this out when things start to feel challenging.

3. **Prepare potential responses ahead of tricky conversations:** Many of us find that our words desert us when we need them most, so planning ahead for how a conversation we're worried about might go can help us think about what we might say, which can lighten the load considerably. I often find a few notes can be a helpful prompt.

4. **Use 'if–then' planning to manage anxiety:** Thinking ahead to potential challenges and what we can do next if they occur can help us to feel less stressed about an upcoming situation.

Knowing that we are prepared if things go wrong can make it more possible to do the things that worry us a little.

5. **Plan and prepare meals ahead of time to reduce stress:** In our family we are big fans of a repetitive cycle of meals and batch-preparing meals where we can. In a highly neurodivergent family, mealtimes can be pretty stressful and finding meals that everyone is happy to eat is hard. Additionally, at the end of the day when we're tired there sometimes just isn't enough energy left to think about meal planning and prep. So we bank the meals that we can and we eat them again and again and again, and at the weekend we tend to do big batches of cooking when things feel relatively calm. It's about finding what works for you, but planning or prep you can do to relieve the stress when mealtimes roll around is likely to be helpful. It's okay if this planning and prep means filling your freezer full of ready meals from the supermarket. It's whatever works for you. I personally find batch-preparing meals a pretty soothing activity to do alongside family members when I'm regulated, but other people may not have the time or might find it stressful or boring and that's okay too.

Reflection

What's working well? What are you already doing? Could you do more of it?

....

....

....

....

What would you like to change?

....

....

....

....

What new ideas could you try?

....

....

....

....

My next tiny step is... What tiny step could you commit to taking today or tomorrow to work towards a different way of doing things?

....

....

....

....

Notes

....

....

....

....

Idea 5: Escape to a Solo Safe Space

Sometimes we just need to get away from it all and spend some time alone somewhere that we feel totally safe so that we can try to find our way towards the middle of our window of tolerance. Early intervention like this can help us to avoid reaching the point of total meltdown/shutdown, minimizing the impact both on ourselves and on our families as we'll hopefully feel able to step back into our parenting role after a little respite. Give yourself a break if it doesn't always work out this way though, especially when you're parenting young children. It can be super hard to stay regulated and almost as hard to find a little bit of alone time.

Five Things You Could Try

1. **Make a safe space at home/work:** Create a safe space you can escape to when you need to regulate. It doesn't need to be big or beautiful. A tiny nook somewhere where you can hide away is perfect.

2. **Agree a signal with family for when you need alone time:** You might feel able to tell them you need some time alone, but when we're feeling overwhelmed this is not always possible. Some people I surveyed said that they would leave something hanging on their bedroom door, or leave a note in a communal family area to let everyone know they were okay but needed time out.

3. **Use big headphones to ward away other people:** I'm a massive fan of BIG headphones as a strong social signal that I don't want to talk right now. This can create a solo safer space even in pretty busy environments.

4. **Hide in the toilet:** Please tell me it's not just me who does this? The toilet is the one place where you (mostly) don't get followed and might be able to take a moment to yourself, so if you need a moment to get on top of things, heading to the toilet and hiding there for an extra minute or two is sometimes the most practical option.

5. **Walk:** Long walks, short walks, any kind of walk can be helpful when you need a little space. If I'm trying to build some space into a busy day I will often choose to walk between the places I need to be (or add in some walking by getting off the bus a stop early or parking my car a little further away). That little bit of alone time between busy moments can really help.

Reflection

What's working well? What are you already doing? Could you do more of it?

....

....

....

....

What would you like to change?

....

....

....

....

What new ideas could you try?

....

....

....

....

My next tiny step is... What tiny step could you commit to taking today or tomorrow to work towards a different way of doing things?

....

....

....

....

Notes

....

....

....

....

Idea 6: Find Family and Friends Who Get It

Parenting, especially for those of us who are neurodivergent, can be a unique journey with its own set of challenges. In this adventure, having the right people by your side makes all the difference. Life feels so much easier when we're around people who understand us, or who are willing to try to understand us a little better. On the whole, people are good and kind and with a little effort on our part, we can surround ourselves with people who get us, like us and help us rather than those who invalidate or judge us.

Five Things You Could Try

1. **Help your family understand your world:** Open honest conversations with your family about how you experience the world and why it feels hard sometimes can help them to empathize with you and give you the space and support you need. This can be helpful for our families too, as it can help to give them a language and safe space for sharing similar challenges they may be facing.

2. **Explicitly thank people who do what you need:** Some people are brilliant. Maybe because they know just what we need and maybe they just happened to get it right. Either way, go out of your way to thank them and explain exactly what they did right and why it was helpful, so they're confident being similarly helpful again in future.

3. **Find your tribe and cling to them:** People like us know what people like us need, so hanging out together (either physically or online) can feel relatively easy and restorative and you'll often pick up great ideas from each other too.

4. **Be explicit about what you need and why:** Family, friends and colleagues are often keen to help but they mostly don't know how. If there are things that the people around you can do to help you, tell them and you'll often find that they are only too willing to do as you've asked. For example, I do a lot of public

speaking and my agent will always ask my host if I can have access to a quiet space because I'm autistic and I need it to regulate. Not only do people always very willingly do this, but it also often triggers further conversations about what else they can do to help. I used to just try and manage on my own, but being open, honest and explicit about my needs has made it far more possible for me to fully engage with my work.

5. **Trust those who are trustworthy:** There are good people in our lives. If there are people who get you and are keen to support, trust them to do so. You don't have to manage everything all on your own and people really do want to help. Identifying the people you really can rely on and being unafraid to lean on them a little on the days you need to is a really positive step. No doubt, there will be days when you're feeling stronger and they need to do the leaning so you can reciprocate.

Reflection

What's working well? What are you already doing? Could you do more of it?

....

....

....

....

What would you like to change?

....

....

....

....

What new ideas could you try?

....

....

....

....

My next tiny step is... What tiny step could you commit to taking today or tomorrow to work towards a different way of doing things?

....

....

....

....

Notes

....

....

....

....

Idea 7: Flip the Feeling with Your Special Interest

One of the gifts that neurodivergence brings for many of us is deep interests or passions. Engaging with our special interests can bring joy in a way that few other things can, providing valuable respite from the world around us. So, when things feel tricky, we can wield our special interest like a superpower to try and get things back on track so we can feel happier in ourselves and a little more able to step up to our parenting responsibilities.

Five Things You Could Try

1. **Find your flow:** When you enter a state of flow, time passes and you don't notice. Suddenly it's dark outside and you realize that hours have gone by whilst you were in your own little world of special interest and joy. It's brilliant. Learning ways into flow can help when we are beginning to struggle. This will look different depending on what your special interest

is and what the flow state looks like for you, but things that can help include:

- access to any equipment/materials needed to engage in your special interest
- books or videos about your special interest
- somewhere quiet where you won't be interrupted or disturbed (I put my phone in flight mode)
- a decent length of time when you don't have to be somewhere else
- snacks – you may forget to eat otherwise, and hunger is our enemy.

2. **Connect with others who share your interests:** Finding other people who share our passion can feel brilliant. Spending time with people you can learn from and who do not get bored of the topic that interests you can feel restorative. I feel this every time I head to the hill with my paragliding friends. Other people may bore of constant talk about the weather, glide ratios and how to find the best lift on the ridge, but my paragliding friends never tire of it.

3. **Diarize regular time to enjoy your special interest:** It can be hard to find time to enjoy your special interest alongside all the adulting that needs to happen. Proactively building time in for it can be an important part of your self-care. This is something I've done with my climbing. I used to find that as life got busier, the amount of time I spent climbing would reduce, but climbing makes me feel good both mentally and physically so now, when I'm looking at the week ahead, I'm always wondering when I can fit in two or three times to make it to the climbing wall. I try to stick to the same times each week, but when that doesn't work (the life of a keynote speaker is never the same each week) then I tweak my diary until I know I'll get my climbing fix.

4. **Ask family to talk to you about your special interest when you're struggling:** When the world starts to slip away and we

find ourselves edging towards shutdown, the one thing we can often reliably manage to talk about is our special interest. Letting family members know this and prompting them to ask you questions about your special interest in moments when they can see you're starting to struggle can be a great way to pull you back from the abyss. In my household, if I'm struggling then family know to ask me a question about climbing or paragliding, my daughter Lyra is always able to talk about snakes or space, whilst Ellie is never lost for words when it comes to talking about her latest projects in Minecraft or SIMS.

5. **Make your special interest portable for crisis moments:** Having something you can carry around that relates to your special interest so you can dip into it at moments when things start to fall apart can be helpful. This might be as simple as a few photos or videos you can watch on your phone. Or perhaps a book, eBook, audiobook or podcast you can tune into. My daughter Lyra is a big space fan and adores Tim Peake's book 'Ask an Astronaut'. It never fails to make her start to feel a little better any time she pops her earbuds in and gives it a listen (mouthing along with the words as she knows great chunks of it by heart after a few hundred listens).

Reflection

What's working well? What are you already doing? Could you do more of it?

....

....

....

....

What would you like to change?

....

....

....

....

What new ideas could you try?

....

....

....

....

My next tiny step is... What tiny step could you commit to taking today or tomorrow to work towards a different way of doing things?

....

....

....

....

Notes

....

....

....

....

Idea 8: Take Time to Reset and Regulate after Trigger Activities

Whilst they'll be different for each of us, one thing that many neurodivergent parents and carers will share is that there will be activities that wear us down more than others and are more likely to trigger meltdown- or shutdown-type responses (see the beginning of this chapter for more on this). Knowing what these activities are is a good starting point, and perhaps exploring whether any of these activities are things you can 'Just Say No' to can help to alleviate the issue. But there will be a whole tonne remaining that you're really motivated to do either because you get a lot out of them or because your personal or professional roles mean that these things simply need to be done.

When we know we're going to be engaging with activities that are more likely to trigger meltdown or shutdown, or take us one step closer to those states, there are a few things we can do afterwards to try and take ourselves back to a state of mental equilibrium and keep us within our 'window of tolerance' and enable us to continue coping (see Figure 9.2). This matters not just for ourselves but for our families too, as regulated parents tend to mean regulated children – our calm is catching.

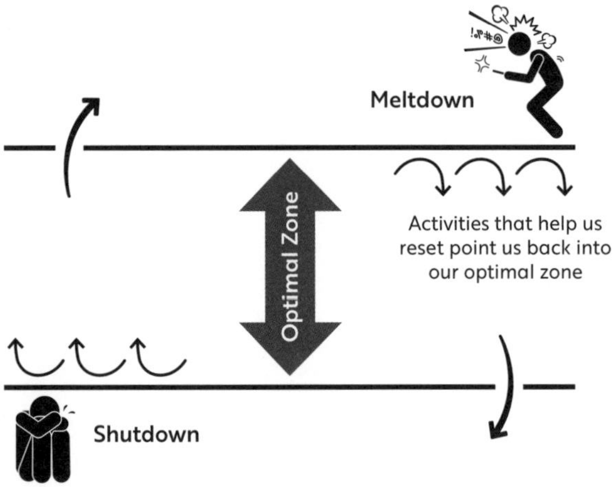

Figure 9.2 Window of tolerance annotated to show how regulating activities can help us continue to cope

When I spoke to parents and carers about the types of activities that were more likely to trigger shutdown or meltdown for them, the responses were very varied. They included:

- talking on the phone
- school drop-off or pick-up
- going to the supermarket
- visitors to our house

- going to a new place
- soft play
- medical appointments
- going to the hairdresser
- social situations
- supporting with homework
- opening mail
- dealing with bills and finances
- taking out the bins (the noise!).

The list goes on. You may find that some of these things are no issue to you or that you've got a whole tonne of your own ideas you could add. The thing is to become more aware of the tasks and situations that are trickier for you so that you can take steps to mitigate their impact.

Five Things You Could Try

1. **Diarize alone time to regulate after difficult activities:** Many of us find that quiet time alone is one of the most effective ways for us to reset and regulate, but it can be hard to come by solo silent time when you've got other pressures on your time. Planning ahead and reserving this time for yourself directly following trigger activities can feel like a luxury you don't have time for, but can mean that you're not forced into taking time out when you enter shutdown or meltdown. For example, I used to find the school run incredibly challenging, so instead of assuming I could get to work as soon as I returned home, I gave myself half an hour's grace to read and regulate. It felt like time I didn't have, but I was so much more able to focus after taking some time out that I began to view that time as an investment rather than a luxury.

2. **Educate your family about what you find hard and the need to reset:** Talk to your family about the window of tolerance and the different things that can push you out of yours as well as the steps that can help you to continue coping. The more your family are aware of what helps and what hinders, the more they'll be able to support and they'll often do so very willingly if only they know you need some help.

3. **Proactively take time to reset even if things seem okay:** It can be tempting simply to carry on if you've engaged with a trigger activity but you're feeling okay. I'd encourage you to take some time to rest, reset or regulate anyway as very often, things will catch up with you at some point. Something as simple as grabbing a quick cuppa after you've made a phone call can help.

4. **Save low-demand or high-reward activities for when you most need them:** If you've got lots to do and can't take time out when you might need to, instead you could try organizing your time so that when you're at a slightly lower ebb you can engage with the tasks that demand the least from you or which you really enjoy or make you feel good or productive. I like to save tasks that I quite enjoy but that are quite repetitive and don't require too much thought for these times, so if I'm working, I might be editing a video or a podcast I'd previously recorded or tweaking slides for an upcoming talk. At home, I might do the washing-up or put laundry away as I like tasks that quickly make things feel tidier.

5. **Spend time in nature:** If you can, getting outside can be a shortcut to helping you to reset and regulate when you need it. Listen for birdsong, watch the clouds or simply stop and notice what is going on around you. Especially if you can get to green space or water, just stopping and watching can open up a wonderful world of nature to us that usually passes us by as our busyness tends to mean we miss out on noticing the birds and bugs around us all the time.

If you can't get outside, engaging with nature by listening to audio, looking at images or watching videos can have a similar calming effect.

Reflection

What's working well? What are you already doing? Could you do more of it?

....

....

....

....

What would you like to change?

....

....

....

....

What new ideas could you try?

....

....

....

....

My next tiny step is... What tiny step could you commit to taking today or tomorrow to work towards a different way of doing things?

....

....

....

....

Notes

....

....

....

....

Idea 9: Have Shared Expectations about Communication

One of the themes that came up a lot with the autistic and ADHD parents and carers I talked to when developing this chapter was the need for shared ideas around communication with our families. Small changes to how we interact within our homes which feel doable every day might include using concise, concrete language, limiting the number of choices offered or accepting that sometimes talking is hard and we might prefer to listen than speak. Integrating these changes and the empathy that accompanies them once other people start to try to understand can have a massive impact on our ability to manage and can also save a whole lot of heartache by reducing misunderstandings. This has the dual benefit of making our day-to-day feel a little more pleasant generally and also of hugely improving our ability to communicate well with our children.

Five Things You Could Try

1. **Discuss how many choices you can manage and when:** For some of us, decision-making and choosing can feel easy sometimes and almost impossible at others. If this is the case for you, talk to your family about how this feels for you and how they can help.

   When it comes to offering choices, this can be grouped into three scenarios:

   - **An open choice is offered:** 'What would you like to drink?'
   - **A closed choice is offered:** 'Would you like tea or water?'
   - **The choice is made for you:** 'I will make you a cup of tea.'

When we're doing well, we might be happy to have an open choice so we can pick what we'd really like, but when we're working at the edges of our window of tolerance, even small demands like choosing between tea and water can feel impossible and can leave us mute and anxious, so sometimes the kindest thing a friend or family member can do is to take the choice away and make a suggestion.

If we don't talk to people about how hard choices can feel sometimes then they're unlikely to make this adjustment on their own as it's standard practice to offer adults choices about most things. I'll sometimes prompt my family by saying, 'I can't choose, you choose,' if that's what I need.

2. **Explore when questions are/aren't helpful:** Like choices, questions can feel too much sometimes. Sometimes we can dive deep and answer all the questions, other times we need simple conversation that demands as little from us as possible. This can be hard as a parent/carer, as kids can be inquisitive. It's worth exploring when the best times for questions tends to be and encouraging them then – perhaps you're great at breakfast time, or the car ride home from school is a time when you feel able to answer all your child's questions.

   If questions arise at times we can't manage them, we could make a note of them and save them for later.

3. **Sitting on the edges:** Many of us can take great joy from sitting on the periphery of conversations without actively engaging. If this is true for you, letting your family and friends know that they don't always have to include you by asking you questions or steering the conversation your way can enable you to quietly observe the conversation and join in on your own terms if you want to. A great benefit of this is that it can enable us to 'stay in the room' and not miss out on what's going on at a time when we might otherwise have felt the need to absent ourselves because we'd have struggled to interact.

4. **Talk about what 'good communication' looks like in our family:** Open, honest conversations as a family can help us develop a shared understanding of what 'good' looks like for us.

   This might include things like:

   - saying what we mean
   - not being too loud
   - speaking one at a time
   - keeping instructions simple
   - pausing for a moment after complicated stuff
   - respecting each other's opinions and ideas.

   What good looks like will vary from family to family, but having a shared understanding can enable us all to get it right for one another.

5. **Take a break after intense conversations:** A little bit of space after conversations that feel tricky for any reason at all can really help us. Whilst other people might be able to bounce between conversations and activities, many of us are pretty deep thinkers who might need a little time to process our thoughts and feelings following a big conversation. It may not need to be long, but a short break to allow us to process and perhaps reset a little can mean we're then able to move on to whatever comes next.

Reflection

What's working well? What are you already doing? Could you do more of it?

....

....

....

....

What would you like to change?

....

....

....

....

What new ideas could you try?

....

....

....

....

My next tiny step is... What tiny step could you commit to taking today or tomorrow to work towards a different way of doing things?

....

....

....

....

Notes

....

....

....

....

Idea 10: Balance Your Boosters and Drainers

Some things build us up (boosters) whilst others break us down (drainers). This is true for everyone and different for each of us, so we really need to find our own path here. But learning to understand what boosts you and what drains you can help you to get these things in balance and to fend off meltdown and shutdown, leaving you in a better place to thrive day to day both personally and in your role as a parent or carer.

Parenting, with its unique demands and joys, can be a world of both boosters and drainers. It's essential to recognize that many aspects of parenting can either fill us with energy or leave us feeling drained. For instance, school events or social gatherings might be draining for some, whilst watching your children thrive in the great outdoors during a nature walk can be a significant booster.

For me, parenting drainers include:

- activities that create mess or disorder
- noisy activities
- going to new places (this feels even harder when I'm 'The Adult' so I feel a need to hold it together)
- when the children were still going to school, homework and school drop-offs, especially if I had to make small talk
- calls from school (instant anxiety, it never ended well).

My parenting boosters include:

- playing a familiar game (we love 'Ticket to Ride' and Bananagrams)
- walking the dog together
- clearing dishes together
- cuddles
- double-Dutch braiding Lyra's hair each morning.

By understanding the impact of various parenting activities on our wellbeing, we can take steps to balance the scales and ensure that we prioritize self-care to recharge when needed.

Now, let's explore some practical strategies to help you navigate this balancing act effectively.

Five Things You Could Try

1. **Understand what builds you up and what breaks you down:** Taking time to stop and think about what your personal boosters and drainers are is an important starting point. We are all different so you really have to do this work for yourself (though others might have ideas to add). But, for example, whilst my husband might find that a beer at the pub with friends is a real booster for him, for me it will be massively draining (that doesn't mean I don't enjoy it, it will just take a lot of my energy and I'll need to ensure that I build in time to reset afterwards).

   Making a note of your boosters and drainers, both within parenting and beyond, can be a helpful way to build on your understanding of yourself and can give you some starting points to share with friends and family too. As you begin to understand your boosters and drainers, dig a little deeper and start to get curious about which boosters work best when. Some boosters work brilliantly most of the time, but when you're right on edge of overwhelm, you might need to go super simple and low-demand.

   For example, I find my Rubik's Cube to be really soothing and it can help me to regulate when everything is just starting to feel a little too much, but the algorithms and ritualistic movements that soothe me when I still have a little bandwidth can feel frustrating when my bandwidth is almost nil. Not being able to cube with ease because my brain is so full can add to my frustration and upset. In these moments, I'm far better off doing something super low demand like cloud watching, listening to a soothing playlist or doing a few push-ups to work out anxious energy. We're all different and different things will work for us at different times. Get curious about what works best for you and when.

BOOSTERS AND DRAINERS

Make a list of your boosters and drainers both within and beyond parenting

My Boosters

- ....
- ....
- ....
- ....
- ....
- ....
- ....
- ....
- ....
- ....

My Drainers

- ....
- ....
- ....
- ....
- ....
- ....
- ....
- ....
- ....
- ....

2. **Plan your week (or day, or hour) with a balance of boosters and drainers:** As we learn more about our personal boosters and drainers, we can try to balance them out, ensuring that when we participate in activities that may leave us somewhat emotionally or physically drained, we counteract this with an activity that boosts or restores us. If you're able to plan ahead in this way, fantastic. If not, then just being aware of the activities you're doing as you go about your day-to-day is a decent starting point. Try to notice if you're doing lots of draining activities and, if so, aim to carve out a little time to take care of yourself with some boosters.

   If our family are aware of our boosters and drainers, this can also help us share out tasks in such a way that the negative impact is limited, because an activity that might be a massive drain for us might not be an issue for another member of the family, so perhaps they'd happily take it on. For example, in my house, if we've had a package left for a neighbour, dropping it round to them and making small talk is something I'd find especially draining at the end of a busy day, whereas my husband or mother-in-law would both welcome the chance to chat to a neighbour.

3. **Be realistic and forgiving of yourself:** Just because other people seem to find certain things easy doesn't mean you should too. Trying to forgive ourselves for having different needs to friends and family is a big part of learning to live well as a neurodivergent adult. If we are realistic about what we can and can't do and we forgive ourselves for having different needs to other people, we're much more likely to find a way of living that works for us and our family and which minimizes the amount of time we spend in meltdown or shutdown. Constantly comparing ourselves to others and pushing ourselves beyond what we're able to do is a sure road to misery and meltdown.

4. **Find booster activities you can do as a family:** Discovering activities that not only recharge your emotional and physical

reserves but also strengthen family bonds can be a game-changer. However, it's essential to recognize which activities truly serve as boosters. It's not always obvious, and sometimes what seems like a booster may not provide the desired benefits.

To distinguish between the two, consider how each activity feels both during and after. True boosters often leave you feeling more energized, connected and content. Pay attention to the sensations and emotions you experience during these moments – the sense of joy, relaxation or fulfilment. These are indicators that an activity is genuinely adding 'currency' to your emotional and physical piggy bank.

On the other hand, activities that don't serve as effective boosters may leave you feeling drained, stressed or even more fatigued. Notice the signs of discomfort or restlessness during and after such activities. If you find yourself needing extensive recovery time or experiencing negative emotions like guilt or shame, it's worth reconsidering whether they truly contribute positively to your wellbeing.

For me, personally, my go-to family booster activities include taking my daughters climbing, going for a family walk, or cosying up with a hot chocolate to watch a film or read a book together. These activities not only make me feel good but also provide quality time with my family, eliminating the need to take time away from them, which can be challenging from a childcare perspective and sometimes leads to unhelpful feelings of guilt and shame.

5. **If things are out of balance, try to take a nap:** Sleep can be a super-helpful tool. If you feel yourself right on the edge of meltdown/shutdown even a short sleep can be an amazing opportunity for your body and brain to reset. It doesn't work for everyone, but for many of us, the chance to sleep, or to quietly lie in a darkened room, can make a huge difference.

Reflection

What's working well? What are you already doing? Could you do more of it?

....

....

....

....

What would you like to change?

....

....

....

....

What new ideas could you try?

....

....

....

....

My next tiny step is... What tiny step could you commit to taking today or tomorrow to work towards a different way of doing things?

....

....

....

....

Notes

....

....

....

....

Summary

To wrap up, here's a quick reference summary of the ideas shared in this chapter.

Idea 1: Know, and Respect, Your Triggers

Understanding your triggers is essential for managing your reactions and emotions effectively. Identifying what sets you off and developing strategies to handle these triggers can significantly improve your overall wellbeing.

Idea 2: Hunger Is the Enemy

Recognizing the impact of hunger on your wellbeing is crucial. Prioritizing regular meals and snacks can help you maintain the energy and emotional balance needed to avoid meltdowns and shutdowns.

Idea 3: Just Say No

Learning to say no and set boundaries is a valuable skill. Communicating your limits to others can help you manage your energy and reduce the risk of overwhelm.

Idea 4: Prepare Ahead

Planning and preparation can be your allies in preventing meltdowns and shutdowns. Anticipate potential triggers and have a plan in place to handle challenging situations more effectively.

Idea 5: Escape to a Solo Safe Space

Finding a solo safe space is essential for moments when you need to step away from stressors and regulate your emotions. Discover ways to create these spaces, even in busy environments, to prevent meltdowns or shutdowns.

Idea 6: Find Family and Friends Who Get It

Surrounding yourself with people who understand and support you can make a significant difference in your life. Foster open conversations with your loved ones about your experiences to create a network of understanding and empathy.

Idea 7: Flip the Feeling with Your Special Interest

Engaging with your special interests can bring joy and respite from daily challenges. Learn how to harness the power of your passions to improve your mood and better manage your responsibilities.

Idea 8: Take Time to Reset and Regulate after Trigger Activities

Identifying activities that trigger meltdowns or shutdowns is essential for self-awareness. Plan ahead to create time for self-regulation after engaging in these activities, ensuring a calmer and more balanced state of mind.

Idea 9: Have Shared Expectations about Communication

Establishing shared communication expectations within your family can reduce misunderstandings and improve day-to-day interactions. Discuss and adapt communication styles to create a more harmonious and empathetic environment.

Idea 10: Balance Your Boosters and Drainers

Recognizing what boosts and drains your energy is crucial for maintaining balance. Develop a personalized strategy that includes self-forgiveness, realistic expectations and activities that restore your energy whilst minimizing potential meltdowns or shutdowns.

CHAPTER 10

Quick Read: Managing Anger

In the journey of neurodivergent adulthood and parenting, there's a shared but often unspoken truth: the experience of anger. The emotional landscape we navigate is complex, and anger, like any other emotion, has its place in our lives. It's essential to recognize that we're not alone in grappling with this powerful emotion. This chapter explores the facets of anger that neurodivergent parents and caregivers encounter, shedding light on how we can harness it for personal growth and positive change.

> **'I am known as a calm person. People often comment on how calm I am. I never correct them because I work hard to appear calm and in control. The thing is that often, even when I look calm on the outside, I am seething on the inside. And sometimes, in private, that anger will overflow. It's not pretty, and I become a walking antonym for calm.'**

Anger is often stigmatized, and we may feel pressure to suppress or deny it. However, through conversations with our community, a different perspective emerged – one of curiosity and understanding. Our anger can be a signal, a reflection of unmet needs or unresolved feelings. By exploring this emotion with compassion and self-awareness, we can find healthier ways to manage it.

> **'I hated myself because of my anger. It was like this other person living inside of me who burst out sometimes. It scared me and made me feel so ashamed of myself. I couldn't talk to anyone about it because I was so fearful of what they'd think if they knew what I was really like. It was only once I finally opened up to my therapist that things started to change. She treated me with such kindness and acceptance that I felt able to talk about my anger for the first time.'**

Within these pages, you'll discover a diverse array of strategies for handling anger in daily life. Some tips offer immediate relief for emotional regulation, whilst others encourage introspection and self-compassion. As you delve into these insights, remember that anger, when understood and managed constructively, can be a catalyst for personal growth and positive change. Here are some tips shared by the community:

- **Get your environment right:** For me, overwhelm often results in anger so getting my environment right is the key to keeping my temper under control. I struggle with noise, so I spend a lot of time with no music and no TV.
- **Don't get 'hangry':** I find that being hungry is the beginning of my unravelling. It's much better if I keep to regular mealtimes. If I start to get snappy and irritable, I'll eat a snack. It's a far more reliable sign to me that I need to eat than relying on the hunger cues that every other human seems to have nailed but I'm rubbish at. If I don't snack when I see these early signs, then my mood can get pretty explosive.
- **Recognize anger:** I'm learning to identify anger: it appears I often misidentify anger as a myriad of other things. Knowing that has helped.
- **Allow yourself to be angry:** These days, I try to own my anger and allow myself to feel and express it. It's there for a reason. I used to ignore it and see it as a lack of control and a way that I'd failed.
- **Get creative with deep-rooted anger:** Since receiving a very late diagnosis of ADHD I had found myself harbouring a lot of anger. I was angry about being missed. I was angry at all the awful experiences I'd had because people thought I was naughty or lazy or stupid. I was angry that the world I'm living in doesn't fit me. So much anger. It was a very heavy weight to carry, and it was largely about things that had already happened or that were out of my control.

The best way I found to move on with it was to pick up my paintbrushes for the first time in years and years and just let my feelings flow through the paint. All the things I didn't have the words for somehow found their way out of me in these massive, ugly artworks. They were far from works of art and I would never have shown them to anyone, but the process itself was incredibly healing and allowed me to find some inner peace.

Yes, I have plenty to be angry about, but carrying that anger with me every day was like a ball and chain and made me deeply unhappy. Now my anger is just something I choose to get out and examine with my paintbrushes every now and then, but the rest of the time I can more or less leave it to one side.

- **Notice and narrate your needs:** Be aware of your stress bucket. Be aware of your own needs. As a parent, you're also managing your child's bucket and you need to both be able to regulate. Notice when you need to step away and have self-care and regulation time. You can help your children develop self-awareness and healthy habits by role-modelling that you need some time and space too. For example, you could say to your child, 'Right now I feel stressed so I'm going to go watch Big Bang Theory,' and later tell them, 'I feel so much better after doing that.'
- **Be kind to yourself:** I used to hold a lot of anger because I wasn't looking after myself or understanding my needs. Blame and shame does not help with that, it makes it so much worse. Wonder, what is this anger telling you? Are you overwhelmed? That's okay. What can you do right now about it? It will keep happening until you look at the underlying need, but you need to approach this with kind compassion. Kindness may be exactly what you need right now; if it's not around you, you can provide it yourself.
- **Work out what works at work:** When I feel angry at work, I try to stay calm long enough to explain that I'm not meaning to

be rude and then I tend to disappear to the toilet to silently scream. Knowing that it's okay to walk away has helped.

- **Use your anger as a force for good:** People see anger as a bad thing, but sometimes there is good reason to be angry. If we can channel our anger we can use that energy, combined with our hyper-focus and resilience, to succeed in making change happen where others have failed. Greta Thunberg has achieved a lot as a result of her anger about the climate crisis. Whilst most of us can't aspire to that level of impact, we might be able to channel our anger to get our child's needs met at school, or to campaign for a fairer workplace.
- **Try to let it go:** I have had to learn to let some things go or they would eat me up inside. It has taken me years to learn to do this and I do still get angry with selfishness.
- **Get curious about the genesis of your anger:** You are human. Anger is important as an emotion to look at. Underneath anger is often anxiety or trauma so look at that. Wait until it calms and then in the quiet, see if that seems different. Often anger is not pure anger and it's a good pointer to what's really going on. Allowing vulnerability is not possible when super angry. Afterwards, when the calm comes, that's where real learning is.
- **Walk away to a safe space:** I often find words are no use, and distance and space and waiting work best.
- **Notice patterns:** Notice how often you're getting angry and if there are any sensory triggers you could try to avoid or reduce. If you're frequently angry, you may be entering a phase of burnout and need to take some time to heal.
- **Make your own rage room:** My kids introduced me to the idea of a rage room, which is a place where you can go to smash stuff up when you're angry. I was pretty taken by the idea and have occasionally created my own version, just using stuff like polystyrene I can punch, cardboard I can tear apart or

water balloons that I can make explode against the wall. It's incredibly cathartic.

In the realm of neurodivergent adulthood and parenting, anger is a shared but often unspoken reality. This complex emotion, like any other, holds a place in our lives. It's vital to recognize that we're not alone in facing it.

In this chapter, you've encountered a range of strategies for navigating anger in daily life. Some provide immediate relief for emotional regulation, whilst others encourage introspection and self-compassion. As you engage with these insights, remember that anger, when comprehended and constructively managed, can be a catalyst for your personal growth and a force for positive change.

YOUR TURN

As we delve into the complexities of managing anger in neurodivergent adulthood and parenting, it becomes evident that this powerful emotion is a shared yet often unspoken part of our lives. We've explored the various facets of anger and how it can be a signal, reflecting unmet needs or unresolved feelings. By approaching this emotion with compassion and self-awareness, we can find healthier ways to manage it.

Now, let's take a moment to reflect on your own experiences with anger.

Reflect on a time when you experienced anger, even when outwardly appearing calm. Explore the triggers that led to this anger and any underlying emotions or needs that were associated with it. How can recognizing and understanding your anger better help you manage it in the future?

....

....

....

....

Consider the story shared of using art as a means to express deep-rooted anger. Have you ever tried a creative outlet to cope with your emotions or find healing? If not, what creative activities might you be interested in exploring as a way to process and release your anger constructively?

....

....

....

....

Think about your relationship with yourself when it comes to anger. Have you ever felt shame or self-hatred because of your anger? How has practising self-compassion and kindness, as discussed in this chapter, changed your approach to managing anger?

....

....

....

....

Explore the idea of using anger as a force for good. Can you recall a situation where your anger motivated you to make a positive change, whether in your personal life, workplace or community? How can you harness the energy of your anger to advocate for your child's needs or work towards a fairer environment?

....

....

....

....

Reflect on the concept of noticing patterns in your anger episodes and the possibility of entering a phase of burnout. Are there recurring triggers or situations that tend to provoke anger in your life? How can you proactively address these triggers or take steps to prevent burnout?

....

....

....

....

CHAPTER 11

In-Depth: Living Well with Anxiety

This is a big chapter because anxiety was a big topic amongst the community who contributed to this book. There was a high prevalence of anxiety, and it had a big impact on the lives and capacity to parent of many neurodivergent parents and carers. Different things helped different people, so I've tried to include a wide range of practical ideas within this chapter for you to pick and choose from. The first thing to remember is that it might feel like you're alone with this and that everyone else is managing, but you're far from alone (as I edit this chapter I'm having one of those days when I can inexplicably feel anxiety humming in every cell of my body. My teeth are clenched, my legs are jiggling and my heart is racing – all with no discernible trigger). There is a whole little army of us trying hard every day, sometimes masking our fears, worries and anxieties incredibly well but often really struggling. As one of the community succinctly and brilliantly put it, 'Every one of us is winging life, love and parenthood.'

Shared Experiences: The Impact of Anxiety

> **'Anxiety is there all the time. Making me scared to just go outside. Worried I'll have a panic attack or that I'll feel weird and spaced out and ill.'**
>
> **'Sometimes I feel outside of my own body. Sometimes my body feels heavy and like my legs don't want to work. Sometimes I feel like I can't breathe or hear or speak properly.'**
>
> **'I feel incredibly anxious about anything I have to do outside of my home. This includes fun activities, meeting friends,**

shopping – everything really. It means I get a sense of dread leading up to any excursion into the world and I extensively think through every possible scenario that could occur. I practise conversations that I might need to have and I try to prepare for every little detail of the event.'

'Anxiety causes me to be hyper-vigilant. I listen out for the doorbell and keep looking out the window (what if I miss someone?). I keep my phone with me at all times (what if that important call comes and I'm not there to answer it?). I need to keep checking my emails a hundred times a day (what if I miss something important?). If the phone rings or the mail arrives or there's someone at the front door, my mind goes into panic mode. Who is it? What's that going to be? Is that the call/letter/person I've been dreading? What if I miss something or get it wrong or say the wrong thing or I'm not available at the right time? What if something I do or don't do impacts my child or my child's care negatively? All these thoughts are in my head all the time.'

'Anxiety is a constant background hum at best, with peaks that are higher and more frequent under external pressure. I only realized as an adult that this is not everyone's experience – I assumed it was normal.'

'I overthink almost everything. I am constantly rehearsing interactions and then replay them in my mind afterwards, questioning what was said, and worrying about what the other person thought.'

'Anxiety has always been a factor. As a mum, it has taken many forms. My children became my "special interest" for the first few years of motherhood and I shut everything else out. My biggest anxiety was something bad happening to them. They were so precious and fragile and I gave over my whole life to them. When things weren't going well, such as

them not sleeping or meeting milestones like their peers, I was anxious and blamed myself.

Nowadays I am still anxious, though have built in ways to help myself and realize I've done a decent job with these amazing human beings, who have become independent, strong individuals. They didn't hit milestones because they too were autistic and developed in their own special ways.'

'Anxiety has impacted my life for as long as I can remember and though I have learned to live with it and have developed lots of useful strategies, I operate with a persistent background sense of panic.'

'For me, it has been life-changing having a diagnosis. There's a reason I struggle, I'm actually not just a crappy parent. It has spurred me on to seek better ways of managing parenting, my behaviour and my child's behaviour. I still get anxious, but I've learned how to manage it and not become consumed by it. No one is perfect.'

10 THINGS YOU NEED TO HEAR

Here are ten things that myself and other neurodivergent parents/carers thought it was important for you to hear:

1. You're not alone.
2. Anxiety won't kill you even though sometimes it feels like it will.
3. Talking to your kids about it makes it easier for you both.
4. It's okay to have boundaries and say, 'No, I can't do that – it causes too much anxiety.'
5. People will help if you ask them.
6. Other people can't read your mind or automatically know how you feel so it is okay to be clear about what works for you. Your needs are important.

7. Anxiety is not your fault and you have nothing to be ashamed of.
8. You are enough. Your children don't need or want an Instagram-perfect parent. They just want you.
9. It's okay to put your own needs first to ensure that you can manage your anxiety and be the best you can be for your kids.
10. Anxiety is one tree in your forest; give the others a chance to grow too.

The Ideas

For each theme in this book, we explore a range of ideas that you can adapt for use in your day-to-day life. These ideas are all inspired by fellow neurodivergent parents and carers who've shared what works for them.

The ideas explored in the following pages are:

- **Idea 1: Don't Neglect Your Physical Wellbeing**
- **Idea 2: Develop Helpful Routines and Rituals**
- **Idea 3: Accept What You Cannot Change**
- **Idea 4: Get It Out**
- **Idea 5: Simplify Your Life**
- **Idea 6: Hide in Plain Sight**
- **Idea 7: Self-Soothe**
- **Idea 8: Curate a Helpful Inner Voice**
- **Idea 9: Talk about It**

Idea 1: Don't Neglect Your Physical Wellbeing

Our physical wellbeing underpins our mental wellbeing, so taking simple steps to boost our physical wellbeing, even a little, can make a big difference to our ability to manage our anxiety levels day to day. Diet, sleep and exercise are the key pillars of our physical wellbeing and we all probably know what we should be doing, but it can be very hard to get it right. Remembering that you're a constant role model to your children can help you prioritize your physical wellbeing. Making enough time to look after ourselves might feel hard, but knowing that our children will copy your example can help us give ourselves permission to prioritize sleep, diet and exercise. I've shared a few ideas here that other neurodivergent parents/carers said worked for them.

Five Things You Could Try

1. **Look after yourself first(ish):** As parents/carers, our physical wellbeing can often fall to the bottom of the agenda as we're so busy looking after everyone else; but if we're to be the adult that our family need, we've got to look after ourselves first. It can be hard to get out of the mindset that it's selfish to prioritize our own needs, but in looking after ourselves we're making it possible for us to look after our whole family. In practice, this might mean blocking out a little time in the diary for exercise, prioritizing our sleep time over housework or saying no to a commitment for your child that might interfere with stuff you have planned to keep yourself healthy.

2. **Banish your phone for better sleep:** Personal experience has shown me that the quickest route to more and better sleep has been to banish my phone from my bedroom. It now charges elsewhere in the house and when I would previously have been doom-scrolling, I'm now reading or sleeping. The result is more sleep, better sleep and less compare and despair.

3. **Plan go-to meals to boost nutrition:** Having to magic up a meal on the spot is tricky, especially if there are different dietary or sensory needs to take into account within your family, or if you're working on a budget. We've found that planning ahead can make a big difference here. We work our meals roughly like many schools do, with a set cycle of meals (we even have a week A and a week B, with a couple

of gaps for planned spontaneity). We also have a couple of 'Go To' meals that can be whipped up in a hurry that we know everyone will eat but which are also nutritious. Our family favourite is jacket potatoes with tuna or cheese and a LOT of salad. Planning ahead, even a little, or simply having a healthy, uncontroversial meal or two that you know you can turn to if needed, can prevent less healthy, but easy meals from finding their way onto the menu quite so frequently.

4. **Find ways to get moving that feel fun:** Many adults don't get enough exercise, but building a little physical activity into our week can both boost our physical wellbeing and also help us to emotionally regulate. Many people are turned off by the thought of exercise as they've not yet found a way to exercise that feels like fun. If you can find ways to get active that also spark a little joy then it's far easier to find the time and keep motivated. This might mean dancing, or walking whilst listening to your favourite music, joining a social team who are up for a laugh if that's your thing, exercising with a friend or finding a sport that excites you. I am often to be found at my local bouldering wall and whenever I'm climbing, I'm smiling. I feel like a big kid and for me, climbing is a pastime that challenges me both physically and mentally. I'm happy at the wall, so I find it easy to prioritize it. Perhaps you could find something active that feels good for you too?

5. **Take tiny but sustainable steps:** One of the challenges when it comes to boosting our physical wellbeing is that we're often acutely aware of what we should be doing and quite what a chasm there sometimes is between this and where we're at right now. This can cause us to set ourselves unachievable goals, or simply to feel like there's no point even trying. If, instead, we can decide on a tiny step that is so small it feels doable today, and tomorrow and tomorrow, then we can make a big difference over time. For example, instead of thinking, 'How can I go from five hours sleep a night to eight?' you might wonder, 'How can I get ten minutes

more sleep tonight?' Small steps feel doable and they're way more sustainable, and we can add to them over time if we feel able to. So maybe, ditch your lofty goals and think about whether there is a teeny tiny step you can take towards better physical wellbeing, that you could start right away.

Reflection

What's working well? What are you already doing? Could you do more of it?

....

....

....

....

What would you like to change?

....

....

....

....

What new ideas could you try?

....

....

....

....

My next tiny step is... What tiny step could you commit to taking today or tomorrow to work towards a different way of doing things?

....

....

....

....

Notes

....

....

....

....

Idea 2: Develop Helpful Routines and Rituals

Routines and rituals can be incredibly helpful in creating control from chaos or in helping us feel soothed and reassured as we go about our daily lives, or a bit of both. What's more, everything feels hardest the first time and anxiety tends to reduce with each subsequent repeat, so doing things in a similar way again and again and again can be a great antidote to anxiety.

Whilst routines and rituals can be incredibly helpful, it's also important to recognize that children, with their unpredictable nature, can sometimes disrupt even the best-laid plans. Finding a balance between having routines and allowing for flexibility is key, ensuring that you can navigate the challenges of parenting without feeling overwhelmed by unexpected changes.

Five Things You Could Try

1. **If something works well, do it again (and again):** Notice when things go well and wonder whether this success can be repeated. What was the magic recipe that enabled things to run smoothly today or left you feeling a bit less anxious or a little happier than usual? What can you learn, what can you repeat? This could be anything from what you had for breakfast to the way you said goodbye at drop-off, or pretty much any other micro-moment in your day.

2. **Develop a morning routine just for you:** What happens when you wake up in the morning? Have a think about what you'd really like this time to look like, especially if you're up before the rest of the family. What's the very best way for you to start

your day and what small kindnesses can you afford yourself shortly after waking in order to reduce your anxiety and set yourself up for a good day? This might mean opting to set your alarm a few minutes earlier so you can enjoy a cup of tea by yourself or an uninterrupted shower or a chance to journal for a few minutes. What helps is different for all of us, but it's worth thinking about what happens as soon as you wake up and small steps you can take to use this time as a positive springboard for your day.

3. **Develop a morning routine for the family:** Taking the guesswork out of the morning and creating a routine that will help you keep on top of things as well as enabling you to feel somewhat soothed by its familiar rhythm can transform mornings. At a time of calm, think about all the things that need to happen first thing, who can take responsibility for what and how long each task takes.

   It's not a very exciting task, but stopping to think about this and consider how to optimize this part of your day can help you get every day off to a good start. The community's top tips to reduce anxiety here were:

   - you always need more time than you think and
   - help yourself out by thinking what might be done the evening before.

   When you prepare ahead, your morning self will always be grateful to your yesterday evening self (even if your yesterday evening self was a little grudging about it at the time).

4. **Use routines and rituals to ease transitions:** Moving between different places, people and situations often feels tricky for us. Developing routines and rituals can ease these transitions and help us move from one headspace or physical space to the other more easily. The more we repeat the rituals, the more familiar they feel and the easier the transition will become. For example, I used to find the transition from school drop-off to working from home tricky, as one

provoked intense anxiety and the other required me to be calm and able to do deep thinking. I developed a routine of running home from drop-off to physically work off the anxiety, then sitting down with a lollipop (soothing) and a book I was reading for work for 30 minutes on my arrival home. I'd listen to classical music whilst reading and by the time the 30 minutes were up, I was completely ready to get down to work. I was doubtful about whether I had the time for this in my day, but the running reduced my commute time, so I won back a little time, and the fact I was so ready for work meant I was super-productive once I sat down to it. Previously it had taken me an hour or more to get down to meaningful work whilst I 'warmed up'.

5. **Little love rituals can be soothing and caring:** Developing little rituals with your family that remind you that you love each other can give you little bursts of love and kindness when you might need them and can feel reassuring for your kids too. Ellie and I have a little ritual that started off as a way to say goodnight at bedtime, but we use it at all sorts of different times of day now and will text each other the emoji shorthand for it if we're apart and want to feel connected. Little rituals like this can feel lovely and special because they're unique to you and your family, so each time you revisit them, they can evoke positive feelings of love, kindness and calm.

Reflection

What's working well? What are you already doing? Could you do more of it?

....

....

....

....

What would you like to change?

....

....

....

....

What new ideas could you try?

....

....

....

....

My next tiny step is... What tiny step could you commit to taking today or tomorrow to work towards a different way of doing things?

....

....

....

....

Notes

....

....

....

....

Idea 3: Accept What You Cannot Change

As parents and carers it can feel like it's our job to fix things and make everything okay, but there are some things that we cannot change. Learning to accept this and to live with the things we can't fix can feel challenging at first, but in the medium and long term can help to relieve our anxiety as we move to a more gentle acceptance of how things are and who we are.

Five Things You Could Try

1. **Try to accept yourself:** One thing we can't change is ourselves and our neurodivergence. We might look wistfully at other parents and think 'I wish' or 'What if', but all the wishing in the world will not grant us a neurotypical brain. Our neurospicy brains bring us many challenges but they do afford us many gifts too, so perhaps quiet acceptance here might look like revisiting our strengths and forgiving ourselves for the things we find harder.

2. **Try to accept your family:** Every parent needs to learn to love the children they have, not the ones they wish they had. Like us, our children are all imperfectly perfect in their own way. With our love, support and nurture they will grow into who they are meant to be. Again, it can be easy to compare our children, their experiences, their journey, their strengths and their challenges to other people's children. Maybe your child is not a piano virtuoso at the age or four, maybe they took their first steps late, maybe they don't want to do their homework and perhaps, despite your love of it, they've shown no interest at all in playing football... Try to let go of all the things they aren't, can't or don't, focus in on the little human you have in front of you, and think about all the things that make them wonderful, just as they are.

3. **Focus on the present moment:** Sometimes, acceptance can be about learning to live with a big, horrible situation that threatens to engulf every moment of our life. Maybe you've experienced a difficult transition or a bereavement, or you're struggling to pay the bills. Focusing on the present moment and giving ourselves permission to find moments of happiness and joy despite the wider situation can give us important moments of respite. This isn't about denying what's happening in our wider lives, it's about saying, 'Things are tough, but right now I'm on the swings with my son and it feels good. I'm going to allow myself to deeply feel this moment and smile.'

4. **Allow yourself to feel negative feelings:** It's also important that we allow ourselves to sit with difficult feelings too sometimes. All feelings are valid, even the tricky ones, and all of our feelings have a valid part to play. If we always look to deflect, distract or mask then we do not give ourselves the opportunity to work through challenging feelings. This will often mean that they'll resurface at the most inopportune moments. If you're sad, or angry, or feeling other big tricky feelings, it's okay and, in fact, healthy to sit with that feeling for a little while. It can help to put a time limit on it, and you might pick your moments carefully, but it can be surprisingly cathartic to give yourself half an hour to have a good cry. I find the shower can be a good place for a cry, or a solo windy or rainy walk.
5. **Act 'as if' you accept the situation:** Fake it 'til you make it is a good route to acceptance if you're finding it difficult to accept the way things are. The idea here is simply to act as if you are totally accepting of the situation and go about your day-to-day life as if that were your reality. What would you think, say and do differently if you had reached the point of acceptance? Try to think, say and do those things even if you're not truly feeling them, and it can be surprising quite how quickly they become your new reality.

Reflection

What's working well? What are you already doing? Could you do more of it?

....

....

....

....

What would you like to change?

....

....

....

....

What new ideas could you try?

....

....

....

....

My next tiny step is... What tiny step could you commit to taking today or tomorrow to work towards a different way of doing things?

....

....

....

....

Notes

....

....

....

....

Idea 4: Get It Out

When we've got anxious thoughts circling in our heads or anxious feelings circulating in our bodies, it can help simply to get them out. That might mean naming, sharing and giving shape to our worries, or working off the excess adrenaline coursing through our system or finding another way. Here are a few ideas to get you started.

Five Things You Could Try

1. **Daily journaling:** Journaling is one of those activities that many of us are aware is probably good for us but very few of us manage to keep up. If you speak to someone who does it, you'll often find they're somewhat evangelical about its benefits; and with good reason. There's a tonne of research promoting the benefits of regular offloading or gratitude-seeking in this way.

   I'm afraid I've become one of those people, though it has taken me a long time to find a way to make journaling work for me. I required routine, structure, simple prompts and low pressure in order to make it work. I journal most days but only for a few minutes at a time. I find this a positive way to start the day and a good way to reflect on what's gone well at the end of the day, as well as to let go of or defer any worries before bed. I've found that I enjoy the ritual of it, and it has quickly become a sign to my body and brain that we're entering the night-time routine and it's time to let go and calm down.

   I've found that having simple prompts to respond to helped me to get into a habit of regular journaling, and doing it at the same time, in the same place with the same fancy pen helped too – but we're all different.

MOOD-MENDING AFFIRMATIONS

I used to hate affirmations, but I have become a big fan of them since using them each morning in my journaling. I pick an affirmation that speaks to how I'd like to feel today (especially if that's very different to how I actually feel) or that reflects a deeply held belief or aspiration of mine and I write it at the top of my journal entry and pause for a moment whilst I try to internalize the words.

I keep a list of affirmations as it can be hard to make them up on the spot, especially on the tricky days. Here are my favourites – feel free to adopt them, or maybe they'll inspire you to create some of your own.

Self-Love and Self-Acceptance

- I am worthy of love and respect.
- I embrace my uniqueness and love myself unconditionally.
- I am enough just as I am.
- I radiate confidence and self-assurance.
- I deserve happiness and fulfilment.
- I trust in my abilities to overcome challenges.
- I am at peace with my past and excited for my future.
- I forgive myself and release any guilt or shame.
- I am a work in progress, and that's okay.
- I am grateful for the person I am becoming.

Empowerment

- I am in control of my thoughts and actions.
- I have the power to create positive change in my life.
- I believe in my own potential.
- I am resilient and can overcome any obstacle.
- I trust in my inner wisdom to guide me.
- I am a capable and resourceful problem-solver.
- I choose courage over fear.
- I am the architect of my destiny.
- I am unstoppable in pursuing my goals.
- I celebrate the progress I make each day, no matter how small.

Gratitude

- I am grateful for the abundance in my life.
- I appreciate the beauty in everyday moments.
- I attract positivity and blessings into my life.
- I am thankful for the lessons that challenges bring.

- I cherish the love and support of those around me.
- I find joy in simple pleasures.
- I am grateful for the opportunities that come my way.
- I am thankful for the strength I find within during difficult times.
- I recognize the value in every experience.
- I am filled with gratitude for my journey.

Mindfulness and Presence

- I am fully present in this moment.
- I let go of worries about the past and future.
- I embrace the beauty of the present.
- I am mindful of my thoughts and choose positivity.
- I breathe deeply and find peace in stillness.
- I anchor myself in the present.
- I am open to the wisdom of the universe.
- I trust in the unfolding of each day.
- I find serenity in the present moment.
- I am here, now, and that's all that matters.

Affirming Relationships

- My relationships are a source of joy and mutual growth.
- I communicate with kindness and compassion.
- I am surrounded by people who uplift me.
- I give and receive love freely.
- I nurture meaningful connections.
- I am a source of positivity in my relationships.
- I am open to love and connection.
- I choose to see the best in others.
- I am grateful for the people in my life.
- I am a magnet for authentic friendships.

Success and Abundance

- I am deserving of success and prosperity.

- My actions are purposeful, and they lead me towards fulfilment.
- I trust in my ability to achieve my goals.
- I deserve positive opportunities.
- I believe in my capacity to thrive.
- I appreciate the successes that come my way.
- I am on the path to fulfilling my dreams.
- I am able to create my own luck.
- I am grateful for the journey and the lessons it brings.
- I am a successful and confident individual.

Health and Wellbeing

- I prioritize my physical and mental health.
- I am grateful for my body's resilience.
- I am at peace with my body and mind.
- I am on a journey to optimal health.
- I honour my body with mindful self-care.
- I choose wellness in every aspect of my life.
- My wellbeing is a priority, and I nurture it daily.
- I am grateful for the balance and harmony in my life.
- I listen to my body's signals and respond with care.
- My health is a treasure, and I treat it with respect.

Positivity and Optimism

- I choose to see the good in every situation.
- I replace negative thoughts with positive ones.
- I am a source of positivity in the world.
- I focus on solutions, not problems.
- I am an optimist, and my future is bright.
- I attract positive experiences into my life.
- I am a beacon of hope and inspiration.
- I expect the best, and it comes to me.
- I see opportunities in every challenge.
- I am a positive force for change.

Creativity and Inspiration

- I welcome fresh ideas with an open mind.
- I trust my creative instincts.
- I am open to new ideas and possibilities.
- I am constantly inspired by the world around me.
- I express my unique creativity with confidence.
- I am a source of creative energy.
- I bring innovation and originality to my work.
- I am an artist of my own life.
- I express my creativity boldly and authentically.
- I am in tune with my creative flow.

Mindset and Growth

- I embrace challenges as opportunities to grow.
- I have a growth mindset and welcome change.
- I am continually learning and evolving.
- I expand my horizons with each experience.
- I am resilient in the face of adversity.
- I am open to new perspectives and ideas.
- I am a lifelong learner and seeker of knowledge.
- I am the author of my own growth story.
- I believe in my ability to adapt and thrive.
- I am on a journey of self-discovery and transformation.

2. **Share it:** There are a tonne of other ways to share our worries with the world besides journaling. When I refer to sharing it, it's not always about actively mulling over our issues with another sentient being, though that can help. It's simply about taking the mush of worries in our head and giving them shape and form in the real world.

   All the time they're a nebulous mess in our heads, it's hard to own or act on our worries, though they certainly do seem to own and act on us. Once we share our worries with the world, whether that's by talking, writing, singing, dancing, painting or giving them shape and form in any other way, suddenly our worries are a more tangible thing. Our worries become something with shape and structure that we can begin to wonder how to manage. Sometimes we can look at them objectively and decide, 'That's not so bad after all... I'm not sure why I was so worried' (I'm looking at you 2 a.m.-end-of-the-world-worries that seem pitifully small and manageable in the cold light of day).

Talking is a very legitimate way of sharing and working through our worries. If it's your preferred mode, think about what you're hoping for from your listener and perhaps share this with them. Often, we just want the chance to think out loud; we're looking perhaps for a little empathy, but we don't always want the person we're sharing with to try to fix or change things for us. I often find talking to a pet can work well if I'm not looking for advice. Or, kooky as it sounds, I sometimes talk to myself in the mirror and do both sides of the conversation, imagining how I'd try to respond to someone I really care about and extend that same kindness to myself. I think this habit is a symptom of having watched one too many TikTok videos with people acting both sides of a two-way conversation in funny little skits, but it works for me so I figure it's worth sharing this little eccentricity in case it works for you too.

3. **Shelve it:** Another way to get our anxieties out and away, for a while at least, is to park them, or to make an appointment with them for later. As unlikely as it sounds, deciding that now is not the moment for this worry and that we'll shelve it temporarily and get it out and dust it off later is surprisingly effective. This can work especially well if you need your whole self to get through a demanding task. Giving yourself permission to let go of the anxiety currently taking up residence in 95 per cent of your brain with a promise to come back to it later can free up a whole tonne of bandwidth to carry on with other tasks. For me, this is one of the joys of journaling

as it can enable me to make a note of, and let go of for now, worries that have a grip on me as I'm trying to get to a point of rest and relaxation before bed. I know they are noted and I can come back to them later. With younger kids, I'll often use a worry monster (a soft toy with a zippy mouth where worries can be safely stored). Either way, putting a pin in your worry and coming back at a more convenient time is often surprisingly effective so may be worth a try.

4. **Shout it:** Sometimes anxiety can leave us buzzing and bubbling. In order to carry on with our regular day, we need to find some big way to get all of that energy out. Literally shouting or screaming (perhaps into a pillow) can feel very cathartic, but other options include running, jumping, smashing play dough or shocking ourselves with cold water (through cold water swimming or a cold shower).

5. **Shed it:** Our worries can feel heavy, but some of them are not ours to carry. Sometimes, we need to identify who should or could carry this worry, either for us or with us. For example, we might:

   - escalate a worry at work to a more senior member of staff
   - confide our worry in a therapist and allow ourselves to let go of carrying it all day every day
   - share our worry with a co-parent or friend so we can tackle it together with someone rather than all on our own
   - write a letter informing or complaining to a company that should take responsibility for something that is on your mind.

Reflection

What's working well? What are you already doing? Could you do more of it?

....

What would you like to change?

What new ideas could you try?

My next tiny step is... What tiny step could you commit to taking today or tomorrow to work towards a different way of doing things?

Notes

Idea 5: Simplify Your Life

One way to reduce anxiety and overwhelm is to simplify things. The simpler we keep things, the less there is to worry about. This sounds really basic, but it can be incredibly effective and the process of removing all the extra stuff, decisions and tasks cluttering up our lives can feel incredibly cathartic.

Five Things You Could Try

1. **Write a to-don't list:** This is my go-to strategy when I'm starting to feel overwhelmed. I take a step back and look at my life right now and consider, 'What could I stop doing?' Are there any tasks that aren't necessary or meetings that could be dropped? I'm looking to lose as many burdens as possible from my day-to-day to create a little more space for myself and reduce the feeling that everything is too much. This requires a lot of honesty and being prepared to be a little brutal in letting go of tasks that might have previously felt important to you. At home, it can mean reassessing some of your standards and letting go of any perfectionist tendencies when it comes to things like cleaning. At work, it might be about wondering whether that report you write every week is actually being used and whether it's really vital that you attend Wednesday's 3 p.m. catch-up meeting or whether, perhaps, you could be excused.

   My to-don't list usually includes tasks that I've taken on for others in a bid to be helpful. I find that I am better at accumulating these tasks than letting them go so it's important to do a bit of an audit every now and then.

2. **Work out your 'MVP' – minimum viable parenting:** Instead of aspiring to be the perfect parent (spoiler alert, they don't exist) when things feel overwhelming, instead think, 'What is the minimum I must do in order to be a **good enough** parent to my children?' In Chapter 2 when writing about bonding quietly and the power of just being there, I talked about my time as an anorexia inpatient and that feels relevant here

too. I was hospitalized with anorexia when my daughters were in infant school. I was absent from our home and I was too weak to even sit up in my hospital bed at certain points. When they'd come to visit, my girls would get into my bed and snuggle with me and I would tell them I loved them. For me, my girls knowing that they were loved was what minimum viable parenting looked like at the time. At other times, different things are possible. But ask yourself, 'What do my children absolutely need from me?' and 'What am I capable of providing right now?' Somewhere in amongst the answer to these two questions will be your MVP. Work out what this looks like for you and try (it's hard) not to beat yourself up if you're not able to achieve more than this sometimes.

EXAMPLES OF MINIMUM VIABLE PARENTING (MVP)

- **Quality time:** Your MVP might involve spending quality time with your child, even if it's just a few minutes of focused attention. Whether it's reading a short story, having a brief conversation, or sharing a quick hug, these moments can be incredibly meaningful.
- **Expressing love:** Sometimes, your MVP is simply expressing your love and affection. Telling your child you love them, even if it's just a quick 'I love you' before bedtime, can be a powerful way to reassure them of your care.
- **Basic needs:** Ensuring that your child's basic needs are met is a fundamental aspect of MVP. This might include providing nutritious meals, a safe and clean environment, or a consistent routine.
- **Active listening:** Your MVP might involve actively listening to your child when they want to talk. Even if you're busy, taking a moment to listen to their thoughts and feelings shows that you care.

- **Being present:** Sometimes, just being physically present is your MVP. Being there for your child, even if you can't engage in specific activities, can provide a sense of security and comfort.
- **Accepting imperfection:** Embrace the imperfections of parenting. Recognize that it's okay not to have all the answers or to make mistakes. Your MVP can include showing your child that it's okay to be imperfect.

3. **Have a meal plan and eat on repeat:** Planning and preparing meals is something many of us struggle with. Doing the planning once and simply repeating it each week or fortnight can massively reduce the stress. It also means you can work out, once, a small bank of meals that your family are happy to eat and which you're happy to prepare. In our house, we work with a fortnightly meal plan and have a week A and a week B like at school. As well as removing the need to constantly plan ahead or think on our feet when a mealtime comes around, this also provides a routine and rhythm that feels reassuring in our neurospicy household.
4. **Manage out peripheral decisions:** I'm a big fan of finding what works and just doing the same thing again and again. This can remove the cognitive load of the huge number of tiny decisions we have to make every day. There are loads of little decisions you'll be making each day that you could manage out if you wanted to. For example, what you reply when asked, 'What would you like to drink?' a go-to answer means you don't have to think about it. Personally, I've managed out the peripheral decisions in worrying about what to wear. Some people love clothes so this wouldn't work for them, but I really don't care about clothes at all – though I do hate it when I feel uncomfortable. I basically have a uniform. I wear the same style of jeans every day teamed with either a white or a black t-shirt (I have multiples of both colours,

in the style I like with all the labels removed) and a comfortable hoodie. I have several different colours of hoodie in the same style from the same brand which I find to be very comfortable. I also always wear the same style of shoes. At other times in my life, I'd have found this lack of ability to express my individual style was an issue to me, but these days, I am grateful to free up a little thinking space and to feel constantly comfortable.

5. **Delegate decision-making:** If you get decision fatigue, let those around you know that sometimes simple decisions feel too hard for you and ask them to decide on your behalf when it comes to little things that can feel big, like what to eat, drink or where to sit. This works best if the person knows you well or you've been able to brief them during easier moments about the kinds of decisions you'd make for yourself. My husband is brilliant at this for me, but it only works because we've discussed it. Many people feel uncomfortable making decisions on behalf of someone else as it could be seen as presumptive or controlling. But if you've discussed it and given your absolute permission, it can feel like a real relief not having to worry about dozens of micro-decisions at points when your brain feels too full.

Reflection

What's working well? What are you already doing? Could you do more of it?

....

....

....

....

What would you like to change?

....

....

....

....

What new ideas could you try?

....

....

....

....

My next tiny step is... What tiny step could you commit to taking today or tomorrow to work towards a different way of doing things?

....

....

....

....

Notes

....

....

....

....

Idea 6: Hide in Plain Sight

Finding activities that enable us to enter a state of flow can help to relieve our anxiety. Easy or repetitive activities which we enjoy can work very well. These activities can help us to 'hide in plain sight' when we're feeling anxious and need calming as they may appear like we're just continuing with our regular day, but we're also giving ourselves a bit of a break and reset.

Five Things You Could Try

1. **Read:** Being able to escape into a different world through a book can feel like great respite from the day-to-day challenges of life. I never go anywhere without my Kindle to hand and will always have a plan for where I might escape to for a few minutes reading if I need a breather. This feels like a totally socially acceptable way of disconnecting from the world for a few minutes and doesn't draw much attention.

2. **Game:** Like reading, gaming provides an escape into an alternative reality. Many neurodivergent people love gaming and it's easy to understand the appeal of a world where you can learn the rules and exercise some control. Whether it's gaming on your phone during a short break or playing games that don't require a lot of time, it offers a discreet way to take a mental break without drawing too much attention.

3. **Craft:** Crafts such as knitting, sewing and crocheting can feel incredibly soothing. Choosing a yarn that feels great in your hands and feeling the rhythm as your needles tap, tap, tap can help you to regulate. These days, crafting is cool. No one will bat an eyelid if you whip out your knitting on the train.

4. **Clean:** Some people find cleaning to be very soothing. Developing some rituals around cleaning and using products whose smell appeals to you can make a difference here. Jobs like cleaning and ironing are probably on your to-do list already, so maybe think about how to turn them into activities that soothe you. This is also the perfect 'hide in plain sight' activity because no one will question you doing a little washing-up; meanwhile, the feeling of the warm water and the bubbles can gently soothe you.

5. **Listen:** Curate a calming playlist that you can listen to if you begin to feel anxious. You can play this through headphones if you need some private time to regulate or play it out loud if you're looking to continue with other activities or to help other members of the family regulate alongside you.

Reflection

What's working well? What are you already doing? Could you do more of it?

....

....

....

....

What would you like to change?

....

....

....

....

What new ideas could you try?

....

....

....

....

My next tiny step is... What tiny step could you commit to taking today or tomorrow to work towards a different way of doing things?

....

....

....

....

Notes

....

....

....

....

Idea 7: Self-Soothe

Learning to effectively self-soothe can help us to calm down and find a little inner peace at times when anxiety threatens to overwhelm us.

ANXIETY: EARLY WARNING SIGNS

Get curious about the early warning signs that you're starting to feel more anxious; these are different for different people but might include things like:

Physiological Signs

- racing heart
- shallow breathing
- unsettled stomach or nausea
- feeling clammy or sweaty
- dizziness
- tiredness
- tense muscles
- trembling or twitching
- dry mouth
- headache

Psychological Signs

- a feeling of dread
- racing thoughts
- feelings of hopelessness
- thoughts of self-hatred
- irritability
- anger
- restlessness
- feeling on edge and easily startled
- an inability to concentrate
- difficulty speaking

As you become more aware of your early warning signs, you can become better able to intervene early and try to take steps to care for yourself so that your anxiety doesn't spiral. Self-soothing can be very effective here, helping you to create a little calm when your body and brain are starting to feel chaotic.

Five Things You Could Try

1. **Embrace your stims:** Many neurodivergent people have stims. These can take a lot of different forms but are most often repetitive movements or sounds which feel good. These are a natural way of self-soothing that many of us develop from early childhood as a self-protective mechanism to help us feel better in a world that doesn't quite cater to our needs. Whilst there are some schools of thought that stims should be repressed and prevented to allow us to look 'normal', I heartily disagree with this and think we should tune in to the ways in which we naturally manage within the world and look to do these things more rather than less.

   We might pick our moment and, for example, hold onto our urge to rock or flap until we're in a safe space, but if rocking or flapping or singing or saying the same sequence of words a hundred times is the difference between us feeling good or spiralling into abject panic then I know which I'd rather go with. Many stims are more discreet, or we can try to adapt them so that they are less noticeable or irritating to others if this matters to us. I do hope we will move towards a time when every neurodivergent child and adult can embrace their stims a little more. They are a brilliant adaptation, which help us hugely.

2. **Stretch:** Stretching can feel soothing and help us to work out some of the tension that can build up in our bodies as anxiety rises. We can do big full-body stretches such as yoga or Pilates-style movements, or we can stretch in more discreet ways, such as steepling our fingers or wrapping our legs around our chair legs. I also find tensing and then releasing

groups of muscles followed by a little movement or stretch can feel good, especially in those areas where we can feel tension and tightness building in our bodies, such as our hands or shoulders.

3. **Breathe:** Breathing techniques are a fantastic way to take control when we feel in danger of anxiety overtaking us. As anxiety rises, our sympathetic nervous system kicks in, sending additional oxygen to our arms and legs, getting us ready to fight or flee. It also reduces the oxygen going to our prefrontal cortex, effectively taking our thinking, speaking brains offline.

   When we take purposeful control of our breathing, both our body and our brain begin to feel different. Taking control of our breathing, in particular breathing in deeply and lengthening our outbreaths, activates the parasympathetic nervous system, letting our brain know we're safe and there's no need to press the big red panic button. It also starts to rebalance the oxygen throughout our body, allowing us to feel physically calmer too.

   There are dozens of different breathing strategies to try and it's important to find what feels good for you. One of my favourites is '5–7 breathing', where we breathe in through our nose for the count of five and out through our mouth for the count of seven. We then repeat this as many times as needed to feel a little calmer. It's superbly simple and highly effective.

BREATHING STRATEGIES TO TRY

These simple breathing strategies involve a long outbreath, or taking command of our breath, and can help us to regain control when anxiety threatens.

4–7–8 Breathing

- Inhale quietly through your nose for a count of 4.
- Hold your breath for a count of 7.
- Exhale completely through your mouth for a count of 8.

- Repeat the cycle several times.

Box Breathing

- Inhale through your nose for a count of 4.
- Hold your breath for a count of 4.
- Exhale through your mouth for a count of 4.
- Pause and keep your breath out for another count of 4.
- Repeat the sequence as needed.

Alternate Nostril Breathing (*Nadi Shodhana*)

- Use your thumb to close off one nostril and inhale deeply through the other for a count of 4.
- Close both nostrils, hold your breath for a count of 4.
- Release the other nostril and exhale for a count of 8.
- Inhale through the same nostril for a count of 4.
- Continue alternating nostrils and repeat.

Equal Breathing (*Sama Vritti*)

- Inhale through your nose for a count of 4.
- Exhale through your nose for a count of 4.
- Keep the inhale and exhale counts equal.
- Repeat this rhythmic pattern consistently.

Pursed Lip Breathing

- Inhale slowly through your nose for a count of 2.
- Purse your lips and exhale slowly and completely for a count of 4.
- Focus on making the exhale longer than the inhale.
- Repeat as needed, maintaining a relaxed pace.

Remember to sit comfortably and maintain good posture whilst practising these techniques. Adjust the breath counts to suit your comfort level, and, if you wish, you can gradually increase them as you become more accustomed to the practice.

4. **Listen to calming music:** Music can be a great way to flip your mood. Curating a playlist of music that you find soothing and storing it on your phone so that you have some musical medicine you can plug yourself into can be a great way to address overwhelm. This has the added benefit, when listened to through noise-cancelling headphones, of helping to block out the rest of the world for a few minutes too.

5. **Create a self-soothe box:** A self-soothe box is just as it sounds, a box full of things that we can use to soothe ourselves. Having a box full of things that either directly make us feel good or prompt us to carry out activities that soothe us gives us an immediate and tangible starting point at times of high stress. This is helpful as when panic means that our thinking, speaking brain is compromised it can be hard for us to figure out what to do to help ourselves. Having a box ready to go makes this a lot easier. You could carry a portable version with you too.

WHAT TO PUT IN YOUR SELF-SOOTHE BOX

There's no right or wrong thing to put into the box. Make it your own and revisit it over time, adding and removing things depending on what's working for you. Here are some ideas to get you started; I use the senses as a springboard:

- **Things you can see:** Pictures or messages that spark happiness, pride or calm.
- **Things you can hear:** A prompt to listen to a calming playlist or sing a favourite song.
- **Things you can smell:** Bubble bath, scented candles, scented putty or pens.
- **Things you can taste:** A favourite food that can be mindfully eaten, such as chocolate.
- **Things you can touch:** Fabrics, stones or soft toys that feel good to hold and stroke.

You could also include activities that you find soothing, such as:

- a favourite book
- crafting such as knitting, crocheting or cross-stitching
- a colouring book and pens
- Plasticine or play dough
- fidget toys
- paper and a pen for writing, drawing or doodling.

Reflection

What's working well? What are you already doing? Could you do more of it?

....

....

....

....

What would you like to change?

....

....

....

....

What new ideas could you try?

....

....

....

....

My next tiny step is... What tiny step could you commit to taking today or tomorrow to work towards a different way of doing things?

....

....

....

....

Notes

....

....

....

....

Idea 8: Curate a Helpful Inner Voice

We are not always very kind to ourselves and when our internal narrative is very negative it can impact heavily on how we feel. Working to recognize and respond differently to our internal voice is a strategy that can take some getting used to, but which can have a huge impact on how we think, feel and behave day in and day out. It's worth trying.

Five Things You Could Try

1. **Notice your negative thoughts:** The first step is simply to become more aware of your inner voice. What do you say to and about yourself? Our negative thoughts can become so entrenched over time that we become completely accepting of them and it doesn't occur to us to try to think differently. Sometimes these thoughts have felt similar for our entire lives, and may have been sparked by negative things that have been said to us or about us.

2. **Question your inner voice:** As you become more aware of your negative thoughts, start to get a little curious about them. Questions you could ask yourself include:

   - Are these things I would feel comfortable saying to a friend or a loved one?
   - Where have these thoughts come from? Whose voice are they?

- What is the evidence for these thoughts?
- Do I want to think these things?
- Are my thoughts helpful?
- If my thoughts were different, would I feel different?
- If my thoughts were different, would I behave differently?
- How could I flip or reframe this thought?
- Would my friend/partner/child/colleague agree with this thought? Why not?

When we start to notice and question our internal narrative, we might begin to realize that our inner voice is inspired by things that have been said to or about us many years ago. In some instances, these may have been fleeting statements which meant nothing to the person speaking but which really spoke to our insecurities and so we've cleaved to those ideas. Perhaps it's time to allow ourselves to try to let go of these thoughts and to think a different way.

3. **Talk to yourself as a friend:** If your internal voice is mean, try, for a while, to talk to yourself using someone else's voice. Pick someone who likes and cares about you and each time you notice that you're speaking to yourself unkindly, consider 'What would my friend say?' and try to hear that voice instead. There is always more than one way of approaching a situation, and maybe our friend's kinder, more compassionate take is one worth listening to for a while. An alternative to imagining a friend would be to take a character from a film, book or TV show who is kind and compassionate and imagine them talking to you.

4. **Use coping statements or affirmations:** One way we drown out negative thoughts and feelings, especially those that feel almost like a reflex because we've thought them so often, is to try to replace them with coping statements. Coping statements are statements, affirmations or mantras that acknowledge any anxiety we might be feeling, but also acknowledge that we CAN do this (see the box 'Mood-Mending Affirmations'

earlier in this chapter for some of my favourite affirmations). Repeating these over and over either in our heads or aloud can help to drown out our negative inner voice and give us a little more confidence in ourselves. You might need to fake it 'til you make it and develop statements about how you want to feel or what you want to believe, even if you're not quite there yet.

COPING STATEMENT SUGGESTIONS

The best coping statements may be ones you develop for yourself that reflect your voice and your situation, but here are some suggestions to get you started:

- I'm anxious, but I can manage.
- This feeling will pass.
- I've done it before, I can do it again.
- I'm capable of doing hard things.
- It's okay not to be okay.
- Mistakes are like teachers, they're how I learn.
- Anxiety feels horrible but it won't hurt me.
- I am more than my anxiety.
- I choose not to engage with these thoughts.

Creating New Thought-Habits

You might specifically pair some of these coping statements with regular thoughts you have so you can try to create a new thought-habit.

For example, perhaps every time you find yourself thinking:

'I can't do this.'

you could consciously try to replace that thought with:

'I've done it before, I can do it again' or 'I'm capable of doing hard things.'

5. **Greet your reflection kindly**: Making an effort to speak to yourself kindly in the mirror is a simple way to start to try to flip the way you feel about yourself. Try to light up for yourself as you would for your child or treat yourself with the kindness, respect and love with which you would greet a friend. This can make an especially big difference if you are usually very unkind to your reflection.

   Instead of bullying yourself, try to show yourself a little kindness and love, especially as you start the day. If you're not feeling it, act 'as if' for a little while and treat your reflection 'as if' you liked and respected yourself. This can become a self-fulfilling prophecy over time and certainly makes for a far more pleasant start to the day than being berated and bullied.

Reflection

What's working well? What are you already doing? Could you do more of it?

....

....

....

....

What would you like to change?

....

....

....

....

What new ideas could you try?

....

....

....

....

My next tiny step is... What tiny step could you commit to taking today or tomorrow to work towards a different way of doing things?

....

....

....

....

Notes

....

....

....

....

Idea 9: Talk about It

It can help to find people you can begin to safely explore difficult thoughts with. I love the phrase 'name it to tame it' because I think that when our anxieties are a nebulous mess in our head they feel totally overwhelming and unmanageable, but as soon as we start to talk about them (or write or sing or draw about them) then they start to take shape and we have something tangible that we can begin to try to manage.

Talking will make some of your problems go away instantly as you realize, when spoken aloud, that this particular worry is incredibly unlikely to happen, or even that it seems silly or trivial once you share it, and you find yourself unsure what you were so worried about in the first place. Other worries will resonate with those you choose to share them with. This can help you to feel less alone and to seek solidarity or advice from those who've walked this path before. Some worries can't be fixed or even necessarily understood by other people, but simply feeling heard and less alone in your worries can be a relief. Being able to untangle the mess of thoughts and feelings in your head with someone you trust can help you begin to explore new ways forwards, even if the person listening acts as nothing more than a kindly sounding board.

Five Things You Could Try

1. **Talk to your tribe:** Those people who get you, who are facing similar challenges and have some commonality of thoughts and experiences will be in a great position to empathize and, if you wish, advise, based on their similar experiences.

2. **Be honest with friends and family:** In Chapter 3, on parenting with a partner, I explored how powerful it can be to be honest in our relationships, clearly sharing our needs with others. This doesn't always come easy though, especially to those of us who are late diagnosed. Many of us have experienced a lifetime of masking, which can mean that our friends and family are blissfully unaware when our internal world is falling apart. A little honesty can go a long way here. Whilst it can feel scary to tell someone we're struggling, we'll often find we're met with love and support. Good people will always want to help, but they won't know they need to if you hide your struggles too well.

   > **'Some days my mum can't bear to be near the world and she hides away. When I was little I thought she was hiding from me, that it was something I had done and that I was bad somehow. I feel bad saying this now because it was never about me and I can see that now, and I know my mum was trying to protect me and never wanted to hurt me... but I think that it's important for other people's parents to know. Children are watching and we care and we always think it's all about us, so maybe talk to us. Tell us why you go away sometimes and make sure we know that we didn't do anything wrong and that this isn't our fault.'**

TALKING TO YOUR CHILDREN ABOUT YOUR NEEDS AND OVERWHELM

When you're a parent navigating the challenges of daily life, there may be times when you need to step back and take a moment for yourself. However, for your children, this behaviour can be confusing and even distressing if they don't understand why it's happening. They might assume it's their fault or that they've done something wrong.

Here are some practical pointers for talking to your children about your needs and overwhelm:

- **Open communication:** Create a safe space for open and honest communication with your children. Let them know that it's okay to ask questions and express their feelings. Encourage them to share their concerns.
- **Explain in simple terms:** Depending on your children's age, explain in age-appropriate language why there are moments when you need some time alone. Emphasize that it has nothing to do with them, and it's not their fault.
- **Reassure them:** Reassure your kids that your love for them remains constant, even when you need moments of solitude. Share your love and affection with them as well as words of affirmation to reinforce your bond.
- **Share coping strategies:** Depending on their age, you can introduce them to simple coping strategies that you use, such as deep breathing, taking a short walk, or engaging in calming activities. This can help them understand how you manage your feelings.
- **Ask for their support:** Encourage your children to be supportive in their own way. They can help by giving you some space or engaging in an activity they enjoy whilst you take a moment for yourself.

By having open and understanding conversations with your children, you can ensure they don't blame themselves for your need to step away at times. Instead, they'll learn that self-care is an essential part of taking care of the family, and they can be supportive in their unique way.

3. **Tell people what helps and what doesn't:** Being absolutely explicit about the ways in which people can practically help, and being honest about the things that make you feel worse, can aid those who care about you to support in the most constructive ways. Many people want to help but don't know how, or they try to help in ways that actually exacerbate the problem. Honest conversations here will enable those who are kind enough to care to channel their energies in the right direction. It will also create a culture of constructive communication that means that when it's your turn to step into the role of helper, you're more likely to be told exactly what to do and what not to do, which, if you're anything like me, feels like a godsend.
4. **Talk to a pet or a plant:** Sometimes we need to get stuff out of our heads but we're not yet ready for the advice or sympathy of others. In these instances, talking to a loved toy, a plant or a pet can help. Your dog will love you unconditionally without ever making trivial suggestions about what you ought to try next.
5. **Professional listening can really help:** The listening ear of a counsellor, therapist or supervisor can provide a safe sounding board for you to begin to explore and move forward. Many of the people who contributed to this book (myself included) have benefited greatly from therapeutic relationships.

Reflection

What's working well? What are you already doing? Could you do more of it?

What would you like to change?

What new ideas could you try?

My next tiny step is... What tiny step could you commit to taking today or tomorrow to work towards a different way of doing things?

Notes

What Do Our Children Think?

It can be interesting to hear our children's points of view so when researching this book, some of the children of neurodivergent parents and carers were kind enough to share their thoughts. Here's what they had to say on this topic:

> **'I get anxiety too so when my mum talks about how it feels like for her and what helps her then that can help me work out what to do and to realize that I'm not the only one.'**

> **'When my dad feels bad and I can help him feel better by giving him a cuddle and telling him I love him, that feels good.'**

> **'One time, my dad told me he worried that I would think he was weak if I saw him getting stressed, anxious or upset. I told him he needs to realize that we're a different generation. We understand feelings better than in his day and for kids my age, wearing your emotions is a sign of strength, not weakness.'**

> **'My mum loves me on the good days. She also loves me on the bad days. That's all that matters.'**

> **'It is better now we talk about it more openly because I am learning how to help my mum and also feel more able to tell her how to help me. We're starting to be a good team.'**

> **'Of course, I wish my dad didn't struggle with anxiety like me because it's horrible, but it's also kind of good for me that he totally gets it and has been able to teach me loads of ways to manage it that he says took him a lifetime to learn and I get to try them all now, whilst I'm still a kid.'**

Summary

To wrap up, here's a quick reference summary of the ideas shared in this chapter.

Idea 1: Don't Neglect Your Physical Wellbeing

Prioritize self-care by maintaining a balanced diet, regular exercise and adequate sleep. Physical health directly impacts mental wellbeing.

Idea 2: Develop Helpful Routines and Rituals

Establishing daily routines and meaningful rituals can provide structure, reduce anxiety and create a sense of control in your life.

Idea 3: Accept What You Cannot Change

Embrace the practice of accepting circumstances beyond your control, focusing your energy on managing your reactions and finding peace in acceptance.

Idea 4: Get It Out

Express your thoughts and emotions through various outlets like journaling, art or talking to someone. This can help you process and manage your feelings effectively.

Idea 5: Simplify Your Life

Reduce stress and overwhelm by simplifying your daily tasks and commitments. Creating a 'to-don't' list and streamlining decisions can bring a sense of calm.

Idea 6: Hide in Plain Sight

Engage in activities that promote flow and relaxation. Reading, gaming, crafting, cleaning and listening to calming music are ways to find solace during anxious moments.

Idea 7: Self-Soothe

Learn to self-soothe by recognizing early signs of anxiety and employing techniques such as embracing stims, stretching, controlled breathing, listening to calming music or creating a self-soothe box.

Idea 8: Curate a Helpful Inner Voice

Challenge negative self-talk by questioning and reframing your thoughts. Treat yourself with the kindness and compassion you'd offer to a friend.

Idea 9: Talk about It

Share your worries and anxieties with trusted individuals who can empathize, offer advice or simply listen, helping you gain clarity and relief. Professional counselling can also provide valuable support.

CHAPTER 12

Quick Read: Low Mood

Within the community, many people acknowledged that they experienced regular periods of low mood or depression. Some were less experienced at managing this and were in the very early days of finding their way, whilst others had developed some great support strategies and ways of managing. The overriding message seemed to be that it's important not to beat ourselves up for feeling low sometimes, but we also don't have to just take it. There are lots of things we can do to relieve some of the pain, or people we might reach out to help us.

Understanding and addressing low mood a little better not only alleviates the pain of day-to-day but can also increase our physical and psychological capacity to parent well. Here are the ideas that the community had to share:

- **Notice it, name it, act:** Don't try to cover it up or be in denial that your mood is low. Don't be scared to name it, catch it and use it to identify what you need. Try to be aware and curious. Why might you be feeling this way? Is there something you need, or something you're lacking? As an example, if I get grumpy around 9 p.m., I might realize that I've looked after everyone else, but I've not eaten. I acknowledge my needs and put myself first for a while.

- **Remember that nobody is perfect:** Embrace the messiness of being a human: perfection isn't a thing. Nobody has their act together as much as you think they do. It's okay to be where you're at; it's a journey, not your endpoint. What do you need right now to get through it?

- **Look through a different lens:** Late diagnosis has helped me massively. It's helped me to view my struggles from a different perspective.

- **Make compromises that enable you to live well:** Now I've learnt more about how to live well with autism, I prioritize rest and sleep, work part-time, set clear boundaries and say no. I try not to be all things to all people.

- **Proactively turn to healthy coping mechanisms:** Identifying my dips early and having a healthy coping strategy helps prevent me from using cigarettes and alcohol to medicate. When I see things are slipping, I make time to do some yoga/Pilates-type stretches or get out for a walk regardless of the weather. My husband has also learned to recognize the signs and usually manages to work out if I need closeness or separateness.

- **Don't suffer in silence with post-natal depression:** Post-natal depression is an illness that can be recovered from fairly swiftly if the right support is sought and received in a timely manner. What support helps people is very individual, but this can include support in the home, support from a psychiatrist or a mental health team, support from a general practitioner (GP) with or without medication, online support, counselling, and so on.

  If you have anyone that can offer respite, then make sure you use this to rest and recover from the birth and to have some headspace AND SOME SLEEP!! Sleep when the baby is sleeping. The washing-up can wait, and use the support to do the washing-up, cleaning, and so on, as this will give you guilt-free time bonding with the baby without the feeling that you are wasting time that should be used doing the washing.

- **Do whatever helps:** Recognize and do more of the things that help you to feel good, especially when you feel your mood starting to slip. These things will be different for everyone so you need to be open to getting to know yourself a little better. For me, it's things like connection, self-care, friendship, reading and quiet time. And coffee. And therapy.

- **Make time for your special interests:** If you're lucky enough to have a special interest, hobby or skill that you really enjoy, make time for it. This time away from the rest of the world doing a thing that feels good can make the rest of your time feel a little more manageable. Having it regularly in the diary means you always have something to look forward to. At first, it might seem like frivolity or luxury, but I've found it to be an absolute necessity if I'm to live well.

- **Get outside:** Try to get outside and move if you can. Nature is really good for the soul. I love wild swimming, it's very therapeutic. I've found that quiet time in nature is the greatest healer when I can't do peopling.

- **Be open about your struggles:** Find your tribe. Be open. I'm only just learning to be open about my own struggles at age 49; my mask was very firmly fixed. I have lived a life on anti-depressants and feeling inadequate and only recently realized that the doctors did not recognize what was, looking back now, quite obviously neurodivergence.

- **Remember the serenity prayer:** The saying 'Grant me the serenity to accept the things I cannot change, change the things I can, and have the wisdom to know the difference' helps me when I'm getting all worked up.

- **Limit your news intake:** My husband has banned me from watching the news in the evening because my overwhelming empathy can stop me from sleeping.

- **Meditate:** When things get overwhelming, I take myself away and meditate using an app.

- **Accept who you are:** Stop being so hard on yourself and accept who you are, warts and all. When you stop trying to be someone you're not, you might fit more comfortably into being the person you actually are.

- **Know who to call:** When I'm really low, sometimes I just need to hear someone's voice, or see their words on text, so I feel a little bit less alone in the world. I might not want or be able to say anything much in return, but just having a friend talking to me calmly can help me move away from the dark thoughts in my head.

  Knowing who I can call and who are the friends who 'get it' and will help me in these times matters. I need to have a conversation with them in better times where they give me permission to call or text them when I'm feeling down, because when I'm deep in that hole I feel like I don't deserve anyone's kindness and no one would want to help me. So I need their explicit permission ahead of time if I'm ever going to pick up the phone when I need them most.

In this brief exploration of managing low mood and thriving as neurodivergent individuals and parents, we've heard a wide range of experiences and strategies. From those who are just beginning their journey to others who have forged effective ways to navigate these emotions, one message resounds clearly: we need not blame ourselves for feeling low at times, and there are avenues to alleviate this pain.

By understanding and addressing low mood, we not only find relief in our daily lives but also expand our capacity, both physically and psychologically, to parent effectively. As you delve into the reflections and strategies provided, remember that you are not alone on this journey. Embrace self-compassion, cherish your special interests, seek healthy coping mechanisms, and nurture your support network. Together, we can continue to thrive as neurodivergent individuals and parents.

YOUR TURN

Now, let's take a moment to reflect on your own journey. How do you practise self-compassion during low moments? What strategies have you developed to navigate these emotions effectively? Have you ever overcome a significant challenge or low mood, and what did you learn from that experience? Consider the value of your special interests and hobbies in improving your mood, and the significance of having a support network of friends or loved ones who understand your needs.

Reflect on the importance of embracing imperfection and being kind to yourself. How do you practise self-compassion during low moments? Note any strategies you use to remind yourself that nobody is perfect and that it's okay to have ups and downs.

....

....

....

....

Consider the idea of turning to healthy coping mechanisms. Have you developed healthy strategies to manage low moods, such as exercise, mindfulness, or seeking support from loved ones? Note the experiences and ideas you have for proactively dealing with such moments.

....

....

....

....

Reflect on a time when you faced a significant challenge or low mood in your life. How did you overcome it or navigate through it? Write about the strategies, support or mindset shifts that helped you during that challenging period and what you learned from the experience.

....

....

....

....

Reflect on the value of special interests and hobbies in improving your mood. Do you have a special interest or hobby that brings you joy and helps you navigate low moods? Share how dedicating time to your interests has impacted your overall wellbeing.

....

....

....

....

Consider the significance of knowing who to call during low moods. Do you have a support network of friends or loved ones who understand your needs and are willing to be there for you when you're feeling down? Share the importance of having these connections and discussing your needs with them.

....

....

....

....

CHAPTER 13

Quick Read: Managing Poor Executive Function

Executive function is our ability to plan, organize, prioritize and complete tasks and it's something that is a real struggle for many neurodivergent people, especially when balancing the demands of parenting. Parenting brings its own set of executive function demands, often on top of the ones faced as adults. This chapter explores how to manage not only your executive function but also your children's, recognizing that it's a unique balancing act.

When we explored this topic, the community shared a whole host of tips and tricks that enable them to manage themselves and their family life day to day. There was also a quiet acknowledgement that our poor executive functioning can feel truly disabling and is something we need to seek to accept in ourselves and to seek help with from others. Expecting ourselves to flawlessly plan and execute tasks because our neurotypical peers make it look easy is every bit as unrealistic as expecting a friend with a broken leg to run up the stairs. Here are some of the tips they shared:

- **To-do lists and alarms:** I couldn't cope without my to-do list. I rely heavily on a calendar on my phone and use alarms to remind me of upcoming events for me and my family.
- **Photograph important information:** I take photos of any letters from school or for appointments and add them as attachments for the relevant date in the calendar app on my phone. I photograph instructions or other important information and keep them all in a file on my phone so that

when I (inevitably) lose the piece of paper, at least I have a record somewhere.

- **Make notes:** I use reminder apps, and make notes after phone calls of what was said. I keep emails for years in case I need to go back to them. I have a Google doc with useful websites I can refer to for stuff.
- **Find trustworthy help with money:** For me, managing money is the most challenging thing about having ADHD and I am still terrible with finances. It's something I need a lot of support with and has made adult life difficult. Other people seem to manage so I felt like I should too, but it was only once I found someone I really trusted to help me that my financial situation started to improve.
- **A spreadsheet could help:** I use my computer to keep Excel spreadsheets for household accounts and dates for all cars (insurance, tax, MOT), house items, and so on. I need some help with it, but I have found far fewer things slipping between the cracks now that I've taken control rather than my old system of ignoring it, and hoping it goes away (it didn't).
- **Do things right away:** I try to pay things, do admin, and so on as soon as they arrive so they are not pending and piling up. Once they start to pile up, they could be there for months and they feel like an impossible task, but most things take a very short amount of time if you're able to deal with them right away. It took me a little time and a lot of effort to get into this habit, but it's been a game-changer for me.
- **Keep track with post-its:** I keep focused on admin and tasks by writing myself sticky notes for what I am in the middle of if I have to stop midpoint.
- **Be an 'executive buddy' to your children:** My daughter colour codes everything for school and keeps a paper planner. I am her 'executive buddy' for schoolwork and sit with her to get work started and done.

BEING AN EXECUTIVE BUDDY TO YOUR CHILDREN: 10 TIPS

1. **Create a visual planner:** Help your child set up a visual planner, whether it's for school assignments, playdates or hobbies. Colour-coding can be used to distinguish different activities.

2. **Weekly planning sessions:** Hold weekly planning sessions where you discuss not only schoolwork but also upcoming events, social engagements and personal interests. Create a comprehensive schedule.

3. **Use digital tools:** Introduce your child to digital tools like calendar apps and task management apps. They can use apps for schoolwork, but also for setting reminders about extracurricular activities or favourite pastimes.

4. **Break tasks into smaller steps:** Teach your child the importance of breaking larger tasks down into smaller, manageable steps. This can be helpful not just for school projects, but for personal interests and hobbies as well.

5. **Set realistic goals:** Encourage your child to set realistic goals for their various activities. Prioritize tasks based on importance, whether it's finishing homework or spending time with friends.

6. **Regular check-ins:** Schedule regular check-in sessions to see how your child is managing their time and tasks across all areas of their life. Offer guidance and support as needed.

7. **Organize spaces:** Work together to create an organized living space that facilitates both productivity and relaxation. Ensure they can easily access their school supplies and hobby materials.

8. **Time management skills:** Teach your child the art of time management, helping them allocate time for different

activities, be it studying, practising a hobby or socializing with friends.

9. **Positive reinforcement:** Celebrate your child's achievements, big or small, in various aspects of their life. Acknowledging their successes encourages them to develop and use their executive functioning skills whilst easing the burden on you if you find these things challenging.

10. **Flexibility:** Be open to your child's preferences when it comes to organization. Allow them to adapt these strategies to their individual needs, whether for schoolwork, friendships or personal interests.

Becoming an executive buddy to your children not only helps them stay organized but also fosters important life skills that they'll carry with them into adulthood.

6. **Build in extra time:** To avoid being late, we leave a longer timeframe than seems strictly necessary to get ready and always plan to be early.

7. **Find work that works for you:** I am educated to a high level, but reluctantly have accepted that some jobs and the level of planning and organization involved are just not possible for me. At those moments I do feel disabled and everyone else seems so much more capable. I'm trying to improve things for my daughter so her adult life can be different. She finds lots of tips on TikTok and implements them. Having a diagnosis is a huge privilege I think because it enables you to move forward and see what you can do to help yourself. It was only at age 47 that I even knew why everything always seems so hard. Before that I just thought I was broken.

8. **Seek reasonable adjustments at work:** Poor executive function is a part of your disability and you have a right to ask for reasonable adjustments at work, whether that's extra time,

things being communicated a bit differently or additional admin support or a personal assistant.

Parenting brings unique challenges to the workplace, making it even more crucial to seek reasonable adjustments. These adjustments not only support your executive function but also accommodate the demands of your family, fostering a healthier work–life balance (which will ultimately make you a better employee).

9. **Remember your strengths:** What you lack in executive function you will make up for in creativity and passion. Try not to beat yourself up for being less good than your colleagues at the more mundane parts of your job; these are not the bits where the magic happens. We need to find ways to stop poor executive function from getting in the way of the magic-making.

   At home too, neurodivergent parents bring great strengths to their families, such as creativity, passion, a sense of fun and brilliant problem-solving. Parenting often involves finding ways to leverage these strengths.

10. **Some days are just hard:** When I have a bad day or I feel dysregulated and full, my executive function issues are greater. Things I can normally do, I now can't and that's okay. Tomorrow is another day. If I can't do something, that's my cue to go have some downtime to relax and recharge.

11. **Prioritize:** Prioritize what really needs doing today/now and do only those things. Most things matter less than we think. Ask yourself, 'What am I responsible for, exactly?'

12. **Create task recipes:** Create recipes of things to do and in what order. If you repeatedly do things in the same way, after a while it begins to feel easier and you are also far less likely to forget a step. Start with step-by-step instructions that you follow each time. After a while, you might find you don't need the instructions any more.

13. **Tell people:** Educate those around you by owning your poor executive function and asking for help. Try too to be gentle and kind to yourself. It's a brain-wiring difference and needs support.

14. **Things change:** It's okay to re-learn how to do life after accepting poor executive function.

15. **We are not lazy:** For me growing up and being told I'm lazy every day of my life has impacted on my self-esteem in a very negative way. I'm not lazy, in fact, I work very, very hard.

It's evident that executive functioning challenges touch the lives of many neurodivergent individuals. From practical tips and organizational tools to seeking support and embracing self-compassion, the community's collective wisdom shines through.

Managing executive function difficulties is not about striving for perfection but finding strategies that work for you. Remember, it's okay to seek help, make adjustments and prioritize what truly matters.

As we navigate these challenges, let's acknowledge that our unique brain wiring also brings creativity and passion to our lives. We may face difficulties, but we are not lazy; we work hard. Let's continue to learn, adapt and support one another on this journey towards a more manageable and fulfilling life.

YOUR TURN

Now, it's your turn to reflect on your own journey. Take a moment to consider the specific areas in which you face executive function challenges and how they impact your daily life. Think about the organizational tools and strategies mentioned in the chapter – do you use any of them, and are there new approaches you'd like to try? Explore the idea of seeking support in challenging areas like financial management and consider how you prioritize tasks in your life. Lastly, contemplate the theme of self-compassion and how it can help you navigate these challenges more effectively.

Take a moment to reflect on your own executive function challenges. What specific areas do you struggle with the most, and how have these challenges impacted your daily life?

....

....

....

....

Consider the organizational tools and strategies mentioned above, such as to-do lists, alarms and digital apps. Which of these tools do you currently use, and how effective have they been in helping you manage tasks and responsibilities? What else could you try?

....

....

....

....

Reflect on the idea of seeking support in areas where executive function difficulties may be particularly challenging, such as financial management. Have you considered seeking assistance in these areas, and if not, would you be open to doing so?

....

....

....

....

Think about how you prioritize tasks and responsibilities in your life. Are there certain strategies you employ to determine what needs immediate attention? How do you decide what can wait?

....

....

....

....

Explore the theme of self-compassion mentioned in this chapter. Have you ever struggled with feelings of inadequacy due to executive function challenges? How might practising self-compassion help you navigate these difficulties more effectively?

....

....

....

....

Section 3

MASTERING NEURODIVERGENT PARENTING

This section guides you through the practical aspects of parenting whilst embracing your neurodivergent identity. We explore how to manage conflicts, handle social events and address various family dynamics.

CHAPTER 14

Quick Read: The Early Days

The early days of parenthood bring a lot of change and can present a particular challenge. This is true for everyone, not just for those of us who are neurodivergent, regardless of what picture-perfect social media posts might suggest. Many of the community who contributed to this book were not aware of their diagnosis during their early days as parents or carers. When exploring their ideas, it was interesting to note the compassion and kindness with which they viewed earlier versions of themselves, despite beating themselves up at the time for not managing perfectly.

> **'I wish I could go back in time and reassure myself it's going to be okay. You're going to be okay. He's going to be absolutely brilliant. You are not going to break him because sometimes he cries so loud you have to walk out of the room to prevent yourself screaming.**
>
> **I thought I had to get it right every minute of the day and I couldn't do that. I got some of it right, some of the time, somehow, and now that tiny boy is the most brilliant man. I have so much respect now for this younger version of me who tried so hard and was actually doing an incredible job, she just didn't know it at the time.'**

The community had a range of ideas to share about how to manage when you first step into the role of parent or carer. I hope some of these are helpful for some of you.

- **Poor mental health doesn't mean you're a poor parent:** This was the hardest for me as I didn't realize I was autistic, I didn't realize my baby was autistic and I suffered with depression. Nobody around me said anything, they buried their heads in the sand like it may go away. There is nothing wrong with not coping, your mental health is not a reflection of how good a parent you will be. Get help. It helps.

- **Recharge:** It's a cliché but you can't pour from an empty cup; you are a human, not a robot. It may seem impossible to get some of what you need in the early days but any recharging you can do is the most important thing you can do. You matter.

- **Routines can help:** Sticking to some sort of routine helped me. At the time I often felt overwhelmed and useless. Looking back, I think I did a pretty good job.

- **Accept help:** Ask for help. You're not failing if you can't do everything yourself, it takes a village. Take advantage of any help and don't feel guilty. If you do not have family or friends that can help, there are some great charities such as Home-Start and children's centres that can support you. Your health visitor and midwife can help you find support too so they are always worth utilizing.

- **Ban the word 'should':** There is no set schedule or timeline or way of working. Meet your child where they are, not where you or anyone else thinks they should be. Ban the word 'should'. Be kind to yourself.

- **Coping with your child crying:** Learn coping mechanisms for the crying. This was something I found very difficult. All that noise that I couldn't control from this tiny human I was trying so hard to help and to love. If there were other people who could take a turn, taking a break from it and finding somewhere quiet to reset in isolation helped. When I was alone and couldn't leave the baby, I would wear ear defenders or listen to music through noise-cancelling headphones, sometimes whilst holding him in my arms, but sometimes I would walk away and regulate and then return to him.

  I found that once I was calmer, he would calm too. There

was no way to find that inner calm whilst trying to meet his needs in that moment, so I had to walk away, look after myself a bit and then look after him. It felt selfish but it was the only way I could cope. On reflection, I think it was absolutely the right thing to do and I should have felt less bad about it.

- **Avoid the 'perfect people':** Don't mix with the 'perfect, one-upmanship ones' as they're likely not your kind of people and they have a special way of being venomous without appearing to be.
- **Find an ally:** Find someone like you who is on the same or a similar path and hold on to them. They are your greatest ally. You just need one person.
- **Find safe spaces online:** Join forums or support groups or pages online that speak to you and feel like home. Seek spaces where you feel you can speak your mind and feel safe.
- **Follow your gut:** Follow intuitive parenting. Don't read loads of books. Don't do all the courses assuming they'll work for you and your child. It just makes you feel awful. Learn what you can about neurodivergence in children and adults. It really helps.
- **Allow your child to develop at their own rate:** Don't worry about the groups and books if they mean you find yourself going against your own instincts about your child's emotional needs. Read up about health and ensure they get the nutrition they need, but try not to worry about developmental charts and particularly (in our case) language development. Allow your child to develop at their own rate – they do not need to feel a failure at two.
- **Share the load:** If you have a partner, set up a routine of shared jobs. Be honest about which bits you find really hard and that you'd appreciate help with. It's easy to assume we all enjoy the same bits and find the same bits hard, but open

and honest conversations about parenting can often help you realize that your strengths are your partner's challenges and vice versa.

- **Have realistic standards:** Don't stress about cleaning. Shop online. Stop ironing. Take a look around at all the jobs that have to happen to keep your house running and which probably felt like a lot to do even before you had a baby and now consider which of them you can let go of or do less often or to a different standard for a while. It's so much more important that you try to keep yourself well and start to connect with your baby than that you wear coordinated outfits whilst sitting in a pristine house. I think it's also important to note here that the only person judging you on all this stuff is you. Your baby doesn't care at all and other parents get it because they've been there.

- **Sleep:** 'Sleep when the baby sleeps' is probably the most repeated piece of advice I was ever given as a new parent and yet I ignored it. If I could go back in time, I would totally do it. Sleep is a really powerful tool to help you reset and recharge, and even a few minutes here and there can make a big difference. If it's possible for someone else to look after your baby overnight every now and then so you can get a full night's sleep, or to take them for a few hours so you can have a big sleep during the day, you will wake up feeling like a different person.

- **Notice and note the happiest moments:** Yes, there will be lots of challenge but there will be moments of great joy too. Try to let these moments grow and allow yourself to really feel them. Making a note or taking a picture to remind you of the good bits can be a nice reminder for the difficult times too. Being a parent is so busy and I think it's easy to be always worrying about the next thing and sometimes, when it's a good moment, I think we need to just slow it right down and no matter how hard yesterday was or tomorrow might be, we should just notice that right here, right now, this is good.

In the whirlwind of early parenthood, it's important to remember that perfection is an unattainable myth. The community's shared experiences reveal that self-compassion and seeking support are essential. No one has it all figured out from the start, and that's perfectly okay.

Let go of the pressure to conform to rigid schedules or unrealistic expectations. Embrace the flexibility of intuitive parenting, allowing your child to develop at their own pace. Remember, seeking help is a sign of strength, not weakness. Prioritize self-care, even in the midst of caring for your child, and treasure the moments of joy and connection.

These early days are filled with both challenges and triumphs, and by showing kindness to yourself and seeking support when needed, you're doing an incredible job on this remarkable journey of parenthood.

YOUR TURN

Take a moment to reflect on your own journey as a parent or caregiver. Have you ever felt the weight of perfectionism or hesitated to seek help when you needed it? Consider how you can show self-compassion in challenging circumstances and prioritize self-care, even in the midst of caring for your child.

Reflect on the idea of banishing the word 'should' from your parenting vocabulary and embracing a more flexible, intuitive approach to caring for your child. Finally, think about the importance of cherishing and noting the happiest moments, creating a treasure trove of positive memories.

Have you ever felt overwhelmed by the pressure to be a perfect parent? Consider how you can show self-compassion to yourself, acknowledging that you're doing your best in challenging circumstances.

....

....

Think about the importance of seeking help and support during the early days of parenthood. Have you ever hesitated to ask for assistance when you needed it? What steps can you take to be more open to seeking help when necessary?

The chapter emphasizes the importance of self-care, even in the midst of caring for a child. Reflect on your own self-care practices. Are there moments when you neglect self-care? How can you prioritize self-care moving forward?

Explore the idea of banishing the word 'should' from your parenting vocabulary. Have you ever felt pressured to adhere to a specific schedule or set of expectations for your child's development? Reflect on how embracing a more flexible and intuitive approach to parenting might benefit both you and your child.

Consider the advice to notice and note the happiest moments during parenthood. Can you recall moments of joy and connection with your child or the children you care for? How can you create space to savour these moments and build a collection of positive memories?

....

....

....

....

CHAPTER 15

In-Depth: Managing Competing Needs within Your Family

You could walk into any family home in the world and you'd find some degree of competing needs as a result of different ages, interests or skills. Within the community who contributed to this book, it was very common to find that our neurodivergent contributors had neurodivergent partners and children too, which sometimes led to a complex interplay of needs within a home. Whilst this could sometimes lead to harmonious needs with everyone benefiting from a similar environment or communication, this was far from a universal experience.

In this chapter, I explore some ways that we can try to create a family life that works for every member of the family, without putting undue stress on any individual member.

The Ideas

For each theme in this book, we explore a range of ideas that you can adapt for use in your day-to-day life. These ideas are all inspired by fellow neurodivergent parents and carers who've shared what works for them.

The ideas explored in the following pages are:

- **Idea 1: Meet Your Own Needs First**
- **Idea 2: Explore Individual Needs**
- **Idea 3: Plan for Success**
- **Idea 4: Enjoy Each Other One-to-One**
- **Idea 5: Zone Your Life**

Idea 1: Meet Your Own Needs First

When living as part of a family, there will always be some degree of conflicting needs, and one of the almost universal truths I've found when working with parents and carers is that we tend to put everyone else's needs first. We're often so keen to meet the needs of other members of our family that we completely neglect our own. The issue with this is that when we chronically fail to acknowledge and meet our own needs, it doesn't take too long before we're in an unfit state to be the adult the rest of the family needs. I would argue that to be a good parent or carer, you need to put yourself not last, but first. By thinking first about how to meet your own needs, you're able to give of your very best self to the rest of your family.

Three Things You Could Try

1. **Understand your non-negotiables:** You may not have stopped often to consider what your own needs actually are. Stop for a moment and think about your non-negotiables for day-to-day life. Once you understand these, you can try to ensure that as far as possible these basics are in place.

WORKING OUT YOUR NON-NEGOTIABLES

Some questions you could explore to try and understand your non-negotiables a little better include:

- When do I feel good at home or with my family? Where are we? What are we doing?
- Are there any smells that I absolutely cannot manage? (You can explore this question for each of the senses.)
- What does my ideal environment need to look, smell, feel and sound like? How much can I compromise on this?
- How do I feel about cleanliness and tidiness?
- How do I feel about bringing other children or adults into my home?

- What things have triggered meltdown or shutdown whilst with family in the past?
- What makes mealtimes more or less manageable for me?
- Are there places I feel I 'should' go with my family that I struggle with?
- What are the bits I love about family life that I wouldn't want to let go of even if I find them hard to manage sometimes?

As well as understanding your non-negotiables it is important to communicate them with other family members so that they can support you appropriately and, perhaps, understand where they're going wrong.

My non-negotiables include:

- no perfume or strong scents
- no surprises
- no sudden loud noises and
- my space must always be kept tidy and clean.

What are yours?

....

....

....

....

2. **Share the load:** Running a family doesn't have to be a solo mission. No matter what the makeup of your family is, you are (or at least have the potential to become) a team. Consider the strengths of each family member and how they might most meaningfully contribute day to day. If you parent together with someone, explore your individual strengths and preferences and explore how best to share your responsibilities.

   Bringing other members of the family on board to help family life run smoothly day to day not only lightens the load for us, but also provides opportunities for our children to learn new skills and feel a sense of responsibility. It enables every member of the family to feel more connected and part of the family team through shared successes.

When supporting children (or partners) to develop new skills or take on new tasks, it's important to remember that they will probably take longer than you, and that's okay. Ultimately this sharing of the load will save you time, but it may require an initial time-investment during the teaching and learning phase. Additionally, you'll need to build in extra time for the task to be completed by someone who's less familiar with it than you.

As they become more comfortable in their new roles or completing their new tasks, family members may introduce their own ideas and ways of doing things. You need to be okay with this before you pass the task or responsibility on. If you're not cool with children or partners having their own take on tasks, explore why and consider what it would take for you to let go. If you really can't compromise, then perhaps there is another task they could take on instead. Being asked to help in a very prescriptive way can result in conflict or demotivation.

3. **Defer until a better moment:** Our ability to fulfil the many requirements of being a parent waxes and wanes depending on our energy levels and emotional and sensory regulation. Try to recognize these rhythms in yourself and defer to a better moment tasks that don't feel comfortable right now. If you're low on energy, commit only to low-demand parenting tasks; for me this might be quietly watching an episode of my child's favourite TV show snuggled up in blankets with them.

   If your child needs a version of you that you're not capable of providing right now, be honest with them and suggest a time when you might be better able to step up. For example, if your child is bursting to talk and talk and talk about the adventures they've had today but your head is buzzing and you don't feel able to listen to them, be honest and say, 'I really want to hear about this, but right now I need a little quiet time. Please can you tell me all about it later, so I can listen really well?' Children love to feel seen and heard by us, so if we're able to be a little more upfront and honest with them in these kinds of situations rather than half-heartedly engaging, everyone wins. Like so many ideas in this book, it might feel a little odd at first, but it can become second nature after a while.

IDEAS FOR DEFERRING ACTIVITIES TO A BETTER TIME

Specific ideas that the community shared for making this work were:

- If I can't listen right now, I ask my son to draw a picture about it so we can keep it to remember his day. He loves to draw so he'll get lost in that a little while. Whilst he's drawing, I regulate. By the time he's done, I'm more able to listen to his chatter.
- I am very low energy by the evening so if my kids want to do something active like kick a ball about, I just can't. When I'm feeling more energetic, though, I love to do this stuff with them, so I tell them I owe them one and we stick a note to the fridge. When I'm feeling up for it, I ask them if they want to play now. We wait until a time when everyone is feeling it and then we'll all enjoy it.
- I struggle with spontaneous activities, but my daughter has a head bursting with great ideas of things she'd like to do. We've come to a compromise where she makes her latest great suggestion and then I put it in the diary for later that week. That way she knows we're going to do it and I'm not having to live my life in a constant state of change or flux.

- I'm able to be fairly straightforward with my kids these days and can simply say, 'That sounds great but I just need to reset for 15 minutes then I'm all yours.' They know then to give me 15 minutes peace and quiet for a mini-nap or to read my book and then they'll get their re-energized mum ready to join in with them. When they were little, I relied on their dad to help me carve out these respite moments. Now they're teenagers and we're quite open about everything, they understand a lot better so I can just ask for what I need.

Reflection

What's working well? What are you already doing? Could you do more of it?

....

....

....

....

What would you like to change?

....

....

....

....

What new ideas could you try?

....

....

....

....

My next tiny step is... What tiny step could you commit to taking today or tomorrow to work towards a different way of doing things?

....

....

....

....

Notes

....

....

....

....

Idea 2: Explore Individual Needs

Family life works best when we're able to understand, and do our best to work around the needs, of each individual. This can mean a little bit of an investment of time and energy at first, whilst we really get to know what each other's needs are and perhaps develop some new ways of communicating with one another. It's an investment worth making as it can result in a far more comfortable environment for everyone. It's an exercise you'll need to revisit over time as people's needs or the environment or circumstances change.

Three Things You Could Try

1. **Understand everyone's non-negotiables:** You explored your own non-negotiables in Idea 1; now it's time to explore the non-negotiables of the whole family. What are the absolute basics that each family member must have in place in order to cope? Are there any places, people, sounds, smells, and so on that are an absolute no for anyone?

2. **Develop a language of comfort and challenge:** Get used to exploring your sensory needs as a family. In new situations, explore together what you can see, smell, hear and feel. Which of these things feel comfortable and which present some degree of challenge for individual family members? Having small, frequent conversations of this type will help to normalize exploring new environments from a sensory perspective and will also mean that as a family, you rapidly become more familiar with what helps and hinders each person's ability to manage.

   Try to maintain a spirit of curiosity in these conversations. Notice with interest that what feels challenging to one child is a non-event for another. Wonder why and how the family can work around this. Try to avoid and prevent any judgemental tones and ensure that every family member has a chance to have their opinion heard and valued.

   As well as helping you to support one another as a family, learning from an early age that other people experience the world differently to them can also help your children to be much more accepting of other people's needs. This is because they'll start to realize that their way is not the only way to experience the world. This is something children do not inherently understand.

3. **Work with individual strengths:** As well as recognizing individual needs and challenges, also consider the strengths and skills of each member of your family. Some family members will feel more able to step up in certain situations than others. Lean into these strengths, giving your children responsibilities that work well for them. For example, in our family, Ellie is very curious about new smells whilst Lyra and myself tend to be overwhelmed by them, so Ellie is the nose of the family. One of Lyra's strengths is that she feels relatively confident talking to adults, so if we're paying in a shop or need to ask for directions, Lyra will often do this rather than me.

Reflection

What's working well? What are you already doing? Could you do more of it?

....

....

....

....

What would you like to change?

....

....

....

....

What new ideas could you try?

....

....

....

....

My next tiny step is... What tiny step could you commit to taking today or tomorrow to work towards a different way of doing things?

....

....

....

....

Notes

....

....

....

....

Idea 3: Plan for Success

Once we've got a better understanding of the needs of each person within the family, with careful planning, we're more likely to be able to ensure those needs are met a little more of the time. In particular, we might aim to get better at recognizing ahead where issues are likely to arise and start to get imaginative about how to work around this. Perhaps, like some of the community who contributed to this book, you've got one child who really thrives on getting out and about and going to new places and trying new things out and you've got another child who only feels safe at home, sticking to the same routine. This is hard, but there are ways to start moving forwards from the deadlocks you may have found yourself in in the past. Here are some ideas for you.

Three Things You Could Try

1. **Consider boosters and barriers:** When planning ahead, whether you're looking into future weeks and months or you're just thinking about the next hour, stop and consider for a moment the boosters and barriers that this experience will bring for each member of the family. Boosters are the things that build us up: they might help us recharge or reset or fill us with joy or energy. Barriers are the things that get in the way of us enjoying an activity: they might be things that drain us or scare us, for example. As you consider an activity, bear in mind what the activity is, where it will happen, who will be there and what the environment will be like. You might also consider how you'll get there and, as you get better at this, what will come before and after, when everyone will last have rested and eaten, and so on.

   At first, though, just focus on the boosters and barriers for each member of the family. Start with yourself and think, 'For this particular activity, what will build me up and what will break me down?' Simply recognizing this and having an idea about how each member of the family is likely to respond to and manage a given activity can help us to work out who needs space to get on and thrive and who will need some extra support in order to be able to successfully access what we have planned.

Where possible, try to plan so that if one member of the family is struggling through an activity beset with barriers for them, the next activity is one that is full of boosters for them. This can all feel quite arduous at first, but it soon becomes second nature, and this little bit of pre-thinking, planning and the empathy it spawns can go a long way towards building a slightly more harmonious family life.

2. **Develop acceptable compromises:** Where there are direct conflicts of need or desire within the family, it can help to build up a bank of acceptable compromises that allow us to enable access to an activity for one child, so they don't have to miss out, without expecting more than is manageable for another child. Things that have worked well for other families include:

   - Bringing the second child with you but allowing them to stay in the safety of the car.
   - Allowing the child who can't join in to use their screens in a quiet corner of a venue.
   - Having an agreed amount of time that a place or activity will be accessed for so that child one can do the thing they love whilst child two knows exactly what the boundaries are and when they can leave.
   - Allowing frequent time-outs or screen breaks for the child who finds the activity harder and may need to frequently regulate.
   - Asking a trusted friend or neighbour to watch over one child at home whilst you take the other out for an activity. Alternatively, you could stay at home with one child while the friend or neighbour accompanies the other child to the activity; this can work well if the activity is one you'd struggle with.
   - Completing the activity directly alongside the child who

is struggling so you can scaffold and support them, whilst the child who is finding it easier is given more independence and autonomy.

3. **Leave plenty of time and build in downtime:** When different people in the family have different needs, everything takes a lot longer than we might imagine. Try to plan ahead so you can always build in plenty of time. When we do this, it takes the pressure off us and we're less likely to trigger overwhelm in our children as we get stressed trying to get everyone ready.

   It can also help immensely to purposefully schedule in downtime or reset time during and between activities so that the various members of the family (including yourself) have a chance to get back to their emotional and sensory equilibrium before moving on to whatever comes next. This might mean:

   - escaping to your own safe nooks and spaces at home
   - a few minutes reading or with a screen in the car between activities
   - a short regulating outdoor walk directly after an activity or situation that may have presented some challenge for some members of the family
   - a chance to run around or get noisy for family members who are sensory seeking after activities that are primarily quiet and calm.

   Get curious about what works well here for you and your family. Building in moments of reset and downtime when transitioning between activities can improve every member of the family's ability to engage more happily with whatever comes next. This can slowly help you to broaden your horizons if you want to.

Reflection

What's working well? What are you already doing? Could you do more of it?

What would you like to change?

What new ideas could you try?

My next tiny step is... What tiny step could you commit to taking today or tomorrow to work towards a different way of doing things?

Notes

Idea 4: Enjoy Each Other One-to-One

We've thought quite a lot in this chapter so far about trying to make it possible to do things together as a family, but there is another alternative, which is sometimes simply not to try. Instead, you can embrace the joy of doing things with just one adult and one child at a time. This is something that surprisingly few people seem to do but if you're able to make it work logistically, the benefits are huge.

It can feel so much easier to ensure that the needs of just one adult and one child are met which, in turn, can often mean you can totally throw yourself into the thing you're doing together. It can also be a great opportunity to deepen the bond between you and the child you're with at the time. When managing the conflicting needs of more than one child, we can be so focused on simply making it work that it's harder to truly see, hear and enjoy each child. One-to-one time makes that all a bit more possible and can enrich and deepen your relationships.

As well as dedicating one-to-one time to each of your children, it's equally important to carve out similar quality time with your partner, if you have one. Parenting often centres heavily around children, but maintaining a deep, enriching connection with your partner is vital. Beyond this, I also recommend reconnecting with special friends and revisiting activities you enjoyed before becoming parents. These experiences, whether shared as a couple or enjoyed individually, can provide a significant boost and rejuvenate you for the parenting challenges ahead.

Three Things You Could Try

1. **Embrace what you most love about each member of your family:** Take a moment to stop and consider what you value, love or enjoy about each member of your family. Think about any other adults in the house as well as the children. Think about times when you've laughed together or got deeply involved in an activity that you've both got a lot out of. Consider times when you've simply been calm and happy in each

other's presence. Try to determine what qualities, skills or passions you enjoy about each member of your family. This will give you a clue as to the types of pastimes you might pursue together one-to-one.

2. **Develop paired activities:** The next step is to do things in pairs. If you're able to make it work logistically, instead of everyone being involved in everything, do some activities one-to-one. Use the ideas that came to you when you were reflecting on what you most cherished about each family member to help you decide what might work in pairs.

   If you're open to it, a good approach can be to encourage your child to ask you to join them in their special interests. If they have a skill, hobby or passion that they absolutely love, perhaps you can spend some one-to-one time with them teaching you about it, or the two of you enjoying it together. Allowing your child to step into the role of teacher, or putting yourselves in a situation where you're learning together, can lead to a lot of laughter for both of you and it's great role-modelling for your child to see you embracing learning. Just remember, you don't have to be good at something in order to let your child see you try. They learn more from seeing how we handle our failures and how we progress in the learning we find hard than they ever learn from seeing us accomplish tasks which we're good at or find easy.

3. **One-to-one days out and holidays:** Big days out and holidays as a family used to be the stuff of nightmares for me as there were so many conflicting needs that felt hard enough to manage at home, let alone when we were away or out and about. Added to that was the fact that everyone had a very different idea of fun and it was a recipe for disaster that was often expensive and ultimately unsuccessful. We've flipped this on its head now by realizing that not everyone has to do everything together all the time.

   The past couple of years, our holidays have mainly been taken in pairs, with my husband and me each taking short breaks with each of our two girls. In our pairs, we work out what we'd most enjoy and simply go with it. I made this work by allowing my children to pick from a list of things that I really wanted to do and which I thought might also appeal to them; after all, it's my holiday too. These one-to-one days out and holidays are so much less stressful than going as a whole family and have felt almost entirely restorative, with very little of the usual challenge of family life. An added bonus is that, whilst one pair is away on holiday or taking a day out, the dynamic at home totally changes too and those left behind also have fewer different needs to meet and can have a relaxed, enjoyable time together.

In our experience, absence really does seem to make the heart grow fonder too, and we find that these little spells of splitting our girls also means that they hugely enjoy being back together again afterwards and have all sorts of stories to update each other on from their brief time apart. I appreciate that not every family could make this kind of dynamic work, but it's been transformative in our home so I thought it would be remiss not to include it as an idea for you to consider.

Reflection

What's working well? What are you already doing? Could you do more of it?

....

....

....

....

What would you like to change?

....

....

....

....

What new ideas could you try?

....

....

....

....

My next tiny step is... What tiny step could you commit to taking today or tomorrow to work towards a different way of doing things?

....

....

....

....

Notes

....

....

....

....

Idea 5: Zone Your Life

Another idea that worked well for some people was zoning their living space so that different spaces could work well for different members of the family, or support them during times of different need, that is, the need to calm or the need to energize or activate. Not everyone has the luxury of lots of space, but even small tweaks and carving out little nooks can make a difference.

Three Things You Could Try

1. **Create personal comfort zones:** Different things will feel good for different members of the family and some of us will need the chance to escape sometimes. If you have the luxury of having a bedroom each, then this is a great place to start.

Think about what this space needs to look like and feel like for each person for it to feel like a safe refuge. My family have been living in our house whilst it's being renovated which has made for many months of chaotic and challenging living. I've struggled with this a lot as I like things calm and tidy and neat. I've managed a lot better than I would have by making sure that my bedroom is simple and uncluttered and clean. It's a space that I can always retreat to and no matter what chaos is happening elsewhere in the house, when I shut my bedroom door, I can escape it all. I like to snuggle up in my window seat and watch the view and read a book – I've found that even just a few minutes of calm can help, especially if I feel on the verge of meltdown or shutdown.

If there isn't space for a room each, then zones within a shared room or creating little nooks within teepees, under tables or in cupboards can give a child a space that feels like their own. Children may need help to work out how to make their space feel safe and comfortable for them and to keep it that way. This is worth a little effort if it gives them a safe retreat. When you're out and about it can also be worth identifying zones or spaces that each child might escape to if they need calming or activating or a little time alone. This might be the car, a garden, a quiet corner or a separate room. Prayer rooms and accessible toilets are often good options for short stints.

2. **Have agreed calm zones and times:** As well as personal space, it can be helpful to agree on parts of your home that are reserved for quieter activities so that those members of the family who need a bit of respite from the hubbub have somewhere they can go to quietly continue. You may also agree times of day when everyone brings the energy down. This can be especially important in the evening as we begin to ready for bed and sleep. It might be that after a certain time in the evening, the whole family engages in activities that primarily calm rather than activate.

3. **Have agreed activation zones and activities:** Similarly, you might choose to have some zones within your home that are all about bringing the energy up to meet the needs of any sensory seekers within your house. Think carefully about how noise and energy will carry from these areas to other parts of your home in order to find the right spot. If you have any outside space, this might be your best bet for a high-energy zone. Don't let the weather put you off. Sensory seekers will often gain a lot from being outside in rain or wind or snow. You might also have some agreed activities as a whole family that can be used when there is a need to get everyone more energized and ready for a more active next part of the day. What works well will vary from family to family but anything that gets you laughing, vocal or moving is likely to do the trick.

   An example from my family would be when we head out to the climbing wall after a morning of learning (my daughters are home-educated) and everyone is feeling rather calm and quiet. We're going to need some big energy to get ourselves ready to transition into the hard work and fun of climbing. Our go-to activation activity in this instance is to put on a playlist we've curated of singalong songs and then sing our hearts out in the car. By the time we've got to the climbing wall, we're feeling energized and ready to work off some energy on the wall.

Reflection

What's working well? What are you already doing? Could you do more of it?

....

....

....

....

What would you like to change?

. . . .

. . . .

. . . .

. . . .

What new ideas could you try?

. . . .

. . . .

. . . .

. . . .

My next tiny step is... What tiny step could you commit to taking today or tomorrow to work towards a different way of doing things?

. . . .

. . . .

. . . .

. . . .

Notes

. . . .

. . . .

. . . .

. . . .

Summary

To wrap up, here's a quick reference summary of the ideas shared in this chapter.

Idea 1: Meet Your Own Needs First

Prioritize your wellbeing as a parent or caregiver, recognizing that meeting your own needs allows you to be the best version of yourself for your family.

Idea 2: Explore Individual Needs

Create an understanding of, and work around the unique needs of, each family member, fostering a more comfortable and supportive environment.

Idea 3: Plan for Success

Improve family life by recognizing and creatively addressing potential challenges and varying needs within your family, ensuring a more harmonious experience.

Idea 4: Enjoy Each Other One-to-One

Embrace the joy of spending one-on-one time with each family member, deepening your relationships and finding moments of connection and bonding.

Idea 5: Zone Your Life

Enhance your living space by creating personalized comfort zones and agreed-upon calm and activation zones, catering to different sensory needs and energy levels within your family.

Reflection

What's working well? What are you already doing? Could you do more of it?

....

....

....

....

What would you like to change?

....

....

....

....

What new ideas could you try?

....

....

....

....

My next tiny step is... What tiny step could you commit to taking today or tomorrow to work towards a different way of doing things?

....

....

....

....

Notes

....

....

....

....

CHAPTER 16

Quick Read: Children's Parties and Social Events

Whether they were organizing or attending them, children's parties and social events were something that many people within the community who contributed to this book said they struggled with. As we explored this, it seemed that this was one of those areas where the pressure to be the perfect parent was especially felt, as it seemed to feel like everyone else attending these events was able to manage better than us, and that other parents and carers seemed to be able to effortlessly pull together perfectly themed parties that were the talk of the playground for weeks to come.

As we picked it apart though, it seemed that images can be deceiving. Many of us aren't managing and often, even with those seemingly perfect parties that looked great on Instagram, there was a lot more going on than met the eye. So how do we make it work for us and our children? Here are some ideas the community shared. Some of these are about managing ourselves and some of these are about making it work for our children, many of whom were also neurodivergent.

- **Prepare for noise:** It will be noisy. Take something like Loops or noise-cancelling headphones – both for you and the kids. If possible, scout out somewhere quiet you can go for a bit of respite if need be.
- **Activate social mode:** Be in 'social mode' mentally. Yes, it might be a heavy couple of hours but if you really want to be there, then making sure you're kind to yourself both before and after, and activating your various masking and

managing strategies just for a little while, can make it possible to make it through. Try to make a plan for how you'll decompress afterwards so you don't burn right out.

- **Not invited? Do something you'd enjoy instead:** My boys were never invited to children's parties from school, which was always difficult when they realized they were the only ones not going. As parents, we were also not invited to many social events with the children. My husband and I decided that if we weren't invited as a family, then we wouldn't attend. Instead, we would take the children somewhere THEY enjoyed, as a family.
- **Plan ahead:** First, gauge if the child wants this. If they do, plan ahead and talk through what will or might happen in advance. Think about steps to help them manage if it gets tricky; for example, find a safe space to move to if overstimulated.
- **Give them space to change their mind:** Remind your child that they can leave whenever they want to, and if they choose to, leave without a fuss. Also, don't worry if they don't want to go in the end. The child whose party it is will still have a great time and your child won't be stressed.
- **Do what feels most comfortable:** I found children's parties really hard to manage. We went to very few but when we did, I tended to choose one parent and just talk to them, or help out by doing jobs (less talking) or staying with my child.
- **Use your strengths:** When organizing parties myself, I've always seen this as a strength. Because of my autism, I tend to plan well and can use this to my advantage. Remember that your party doesn't have to be like anyone else's and if you take steps to make you and your child happy and comfortable then it's likely that everyone else will be happy and comfortable too.

- **Don't assume your child wants a party:** We spent years organizing parties for our daughters. It was so stressful and cost us a fortune. When they were a bit bigger, they confided in us that they would really rather just have a special family day, so we started doing that instead. We just let the kids set the agenda for the day and tried to create a situation in which we could have fun in a way that worked for our family. No more parties turned out to be a relief for all of us... I wish we'd had the conversation sooner.

- **Just leave:** When you get to the point where you want to leave an event, just leave. Often saying goodbye can take ages and involves a whole new round of small talk which can take you from the point of just about managing to no longer managing at all. Quit whilst you're ahead and quietly exit stage left. You can always drop the host a note to say thanks via text later.

- **Plan for a post-party rest:** Children's parties and social events can be particularly draining for neurodivergent parents and our children. To make the experience more manageable, consider planning for a rest period after the event. This could involve setting aside a quiet space at home or a nearby location where you and your child can decompress. Allocate time for rest, whether it's a short nap, quiet reading or engaging in a calming activity. This proactive step ensures that you and your child have a chance to recharge and recover from the sensory and social demands of the party.

As we've delved into the realm of children's parties and social gatherings, it's evident that these situations can be particularly challenging for many parents and children alike, especially within the neurodivergent community. The pressure to conform to social norms can be overwhelming, but it's essential to remember that appearances can be deceiving. Behind the façade of picture-perfect parties often lie hidden complexities.

Our community has shared valuable insights for navigating these social waters. By preparing for sensory challenges, both for yourself and your child, and activating your 'social mode', you can make these events more manageable. It's crucial to prioritize your mental wellbeing and plan for decompression after the event. Additionally, consider alternative plans if your child isn't invited to parties, aligning with their interests. Communication and preparation are key to supporting your child's social experiences. Most importantly, respect your child's desires and comfort levels when it comes to parties and gatherings, even if it means departing early. Embracing these strategies can help you create more positive social experiences for you and your child.

YOUR TURN

Now, it's your turn to reflect on your own experiences and challenges. Think about your child's sensitivity to noise and how you cope with it. Are you prepared with the right tools to accommodate sensory needs during social events? Consider your mental preparation and how you transition into 'social mode'. What strategies can you employ to make these gatherings less overwhelming? You can explore these questions and more using the following prompts.

Reflect on your child's sensitivity to noise and your own coping mechanisms. Are you prepared with tools like noise-cancelling headphones or a quiet space for respite when attending noisy events? How can you better accommodate you or your child's sensory needs in social settings?

....

....

....

....

Consider your mental preparation for social events. How do you transition into 'social mode' and manage the challenges that come with it? Reflect on strategies to make social gatherings more manageable for both you and your child, as well as ways to decompress afterwards.

Reflect on your approach to social invitations for your child and family. If your child is not invited to events or parties, do you have alternative plans that they would enjoy? How can you prioritize family activities that align with your child's interests and preferences?

Think about how you plan for social events involving your child. Do you discuss what might happen in advance and have a plan to help them manage if things become overwhelming? Reflect on ways to support your child's social experiences through clear communication and preparation.

Consider your child's desires regarding parties and social events. Are you assuming they want a traditional party, or have you discussed their preferences? Reflect on the importance of respecting your child's comfort and choices, even if it means opting for alternative celebrations or leaving events early.

Section 4

FINDING JOY

This final section is dedicated to helping you find joy in your parenting. We'll explore the pleasure to be found in embracing our authentic selves, hunt for the everyday joys that parenting can bring and consider how to celebrate the positives whilst reframing the negatives. The book ends with heart-warming stories from fellow parents, all echoing the resounding theme of joy in the beautiful chaos of neurodivergent family life.

CHAPTER 17

Quick Read: Finding Joy in Being You

Before we can successfully guide the next generation, we must embark on our own journey of self-discovery.

As parents and caregivers, we often find ourselves pouring boundless love and understanding into our children, celebrating their quirks and unique perspectives. Yet I've personally experienced the struggle of extending the same compassion and acceptance to myself as a neurodivergent individual. This chapter is dedicated to the art of self-compassion and the joy that arises from fully embracing our neurodivergent selves.

Throughout my research and conversations with the neurodivergent community, I've encountered a shared sentiment of uncertainty. Many individuals, including myself, have faced challenges when it comes to accepting and loving ourselves. This chapter is a testament to the idea that self-compassion is a cornerstone for resilient parenting and a happier, more fulfilled life.

This journey of self-identity doesn't unfold hastily; it's a process that continually evolves as we live, learn and laugh alongside our children. With the wisdom and insights shared in this chapter, you'll find guidance on becoming more confident and comfortable with your place in the world. It's a journey of self-parenting, a dedication to nurturing the caregiver within.

By embracing your neurodivergent diagnosis and identity, you'll discover that this isn't just a journey of self-acceptance; it's a journey towards joy. Each piece of advice from the community provides a stepping stone towards self-discovery, and, collectively, they form a path to finding the pleasure in being authentically you.

Here's the advice that the community had to share about embracing our true selves:

- **Be kind to yourself:** When my eldest was diagnosed the penny dropped for me. I am so much kinder to myself now. My whole life I thought I was a defective human being and now I realize I'm autistic and that has been truly freeing. My life has definitely transformed in a really positive way.
- **Learn what you can:** It's incredibly validating to hear other people's experiences – social media has so many wonderful neurodivergent people raising awareness. Let this be your own journey, there is no right or wrong.
- **Look ahead:** If you're not embracing it, that's okay. It can feel scary and frustrating; you might mourn the 'what could have been' if you'd known earlier, but try not to get stuck there. Recognize how the diagnosis can support you in thriving in your journey ahead.
- **Drop the mask:** Dropping the mask can be fun – if you need to stand up during long meetings, for example, but never dared before, you now know there's a reason you need to, and people should be accepting of that.
- **Use your journey to help make your children's easier:** Diagnosis can help make sense of your life and you can use it to transform your children's lives too. My daughter will hopefully have an easier and different life to mine, where she is proud of herself. Diagnosis and understanding can be a gift.
- **Accept help:** Get therapy. I was adrift until I sought help and now I feel so much more able to unmask and set boundaries I've previously not put in place regarding my needs.
- **Forgive yourself:** Self-forgiveness is a beautiful thing, embrace it.
- **You're doing okay:** All my life I thought I was a rubbish person – I always struggled to cope. At 49 I was diagnosed autistic and now I realize that even though I am a rubbish neurotypical person, as an autistic person I am doing okay. I am much

kinder to myself, I give myself time and space to breathe and I am working on the mum guilt.

- **Be yourself:** Learning that you're neurodivergent doesn't change who you fundamentally are. You've always been you. Try to allow this deeper understanding of self to allow you to be more, rather than less, you.
- **Try to flip bitter feelings into lessons learned:** Don't think of the years as wasted. Look back and think, 'Well, these things make more sense now.' Try not to get angry over what could have been. Think, 'Well, I learnt some things the hard way and I now understand.'
- **Have fun with it:** It helps that I'm happy to joke about it! I find myself saying things like 'Spot the autistic in the room' when I realize I've organized things way more carefully than most people would, or 'If you ask your autistic friend a question, expect an honest answer,' when I realize I've just been way more blunt in my answer than my friend might have been hoping for. Joking about it is helping me to notice the ways in which I'm different and is kind of a way of educating both myself and those around me about the slightly different path I tread without me trying to constantly bend and change to fit the world their way. It works for me. I guess the thing is to make sure it stays comfortable and never descends into teasing or mockery or shame.
- **Support yourself as you'd support a child:** I've tried to approach managing myself and resolving arguments in the same way I would with a neurodivergent child, and found this has really helped. For example:
  - I take a few minutes to myself before I get out of the car.
  - I go to a quiet room when I'm feeling stressed.
  - I let people know what I need – verbalizing things such as 'How long do you think you'll be staying? I need to know.'

- **Find your tribe:** You might feel totally alone, but there are lots of people out there like you – you just need to find them. It's one of the things I learned contributing to this book. I honestly thought I was the only one fighting these exact battles, but every time I share a problem in the group, maybe a little bit ashamed or embarrassed because surely everyone else is getting this right, I'm met with a bunch of 'Me too!'s and I feel this huge sense of relief.

- **Get curious about yourself:** Realizing you're neurodivergent, whether that's through formal diagnosis or self-identifying, it's like being handed a different key to your own life. You can suddenly open a different door and realize that so many things you do, think and feel are that way because you are neurodivergent. There's a reason why some stuff is hard and why you're so much better at some things than other people. It's an exciting journey of self-discovery. Get curious about who you are and how you can embrace the good bits and learn to better manage the bits of life that feel harder for you. As well as helping you carve a better life out for yourself, this will also make you an excellent role model to your children, who'll learn first hand how, and why, to live life with curiosity and authenticity.

- **Own it:** Own your identity as you feel it. In your day-to-day life, no one is going to ask for a piece of paper to prove you're for real. Just say it loud, say it clear and put your best foot forwards.

- **Be patient:** When the friend who has known you forever says, 'But you can't be autistic because you maintain eye contact / have a job / have a partner (delete as applicable)' try not to punch them. Instead, this is the chance to start to gently explain just how hard you've been working every day to do this stuff and the toll it has taken on you.

- **Educate or walk away:** It shouldn't be our job to educate others about neurodivergence but, along the way, you'll be misunderstood, dismissed and questioned. Sometimes people are open to learning about our experience; if you have the energy, educate them. Some people are closed-minded or unkind. With them, I'd advise simply walking away to protect yourself. The problem is with them, not you.

- **Make careful use of your new neurodar:** As you learn more about yourself and your neurodivergence, you'll suddenly start noticing it in the people around you. You'll be diagnosing your old history teacher, your dad, your best friend's cousin's daughter, the guy who serves you at the petrol station... It's kind of everywhere and can become a bit of a special interest as we dive deep into the journey of discovery. The thing is that not everyone is ready to explore their potential neurodivergence, so if you don't want to upset people, tread carefully with how much and with whom you share your new diagnostic superpowers.

It's common as a parent or carer trying to get it right, to focus your attention solely on your children, but it's important that you first shine the light on yourself and take steps to become a little more comfortable in your neurodivergent identity and your place in the world. As well as being an important form of self-care that will contribute to you feeling physically and psychologically strong enough to be the parent your kids need, you'll also be an excellent guide to your children. We desperately hope for our children to develop self-compassion and self-acceptance; they can and they will, especially if we show them the way by working hard to learn to love ourselves a little more.

YOUR TURN

Now, it's your turn to embark on a journey of self-reflection and exploration. Take a moment to ponder how the recognition of your own neurodivergence or late diagnosis has influenced your self-perception. Has it sparked any profound shifts in the way you view yourself, opening doors to self-compassion and acceptance you may not have previously explored? Share your personal insights and experiences as you consider the path you've travelled in discovering your unique identity.

How has the recognition of your own neurodivergence or late diagnosis affected your self-perception? Reflect on any significant shifts in your self-view.

....

....

....

....

Share a personal experience where you dropped the mask and embraced your neurodivergent traits. How did it feel, and what was the outcome?

....

....

....

....

Explore the idea of using your journey of self-discovery to benefit your children. How can your own self-compassion and self-acceptance influence the way you guide your children on their neurodivergent paths?

....

....

....

....

Think about the people in your life who have been supportive of your neurodivergent identity. How have their understanding and empathy impacted your journey?

....

....

....

....

Consider the concept of educating or walking away when faced with misunderstanding or dismissal. Can you recall a specific situation where you chose one of these approaches? What were the results?

....

....

....

....

CHAPTER 18

Quick Read: Everyday Parenting Pleasures

Parenting is a journey filled with countless precious moments that often go unnoticed in the hustle and bustle of daily life. Learning to seek and find joy in ordinary day-to-day activities can give us a little boost when we might most need it. In the midst of changing nappies, preparing meals and juggling schedules, there's a treasure trove of joy waiting to be discovered. These simple pleasures, like buttoning up a shirt for the first time, sharing a meal or enjoying a cosy movie night, are the heart-warming threads that weave the tapestry of parenthood, if only we look for those threads.

This is something I've found powerful in my own parenting. Noticing the joy in the everyday is something I try to microdose on; a little joy here and there can be enough to help me make it through the day. For example, this week I've found moments of joy in:

- seeing Ellie heartily tuck into a plate of macaroni cheese that my mother-in-law made for her because it's her favourite
- seeing Lyra light up when I told her how proud I was of her for completing an English assignment with very little input from me
- laughing about the state of the kitchen after my children made cookies together and making a game of tidying up rather than going straight into stressed-out nagging mode (this required effort but was worth it)
- watching the sunrise with Ellie
- basking in my daughters' pride when I parallel parked the

car beautifully (this is not a strength of mine and I often go to great lengths to avoid even trying)

- flopping into my husband's arms and letting his love engulf me at the end of a very anxious day
- enjoying the smell and feel of my favourite soap as I lathered up in the shower at the end of the day
- the sound of Mork's purr and the feel of her paws massaging my leg as I'm trying to focus on writing this.

As a neurodivergent parent, each day can be a challenge, but each day is also an opportunity to find joy in the little things too – to savour the tastes, sounds and experiences that make parenting an extraordinary adventure.

When I asked neurodivergent parents about their everyday parenting pleasures, here are the simple pleasures they chose to share:

- **Morning cuddles:** Starting the day with warm, snuggly hugs is something that never gets old for me. It's a simple pleasure that sets a positive tone for the day.
- **Taste appreciation:** On the days when we're able to eat as a family and everyone is in a relatively good mood, I make a conscious effort to I try to savour every bite of the meal we're sharing together. The joy of good food and quality time around the table is heart-warming.
- **TV show bonding:** Watching a favourite TV show together as a family is something that makes us smile. The joy of shared laughter and cosy moments on the sofa watching a familiar show for the umpteenth time is a precious bonding experience that feels manageable even when most other things would feel too much.
- **Storytelling adventures:** We like to make up stories before bedtime. Weaving tales together and getting lost in the magic of storytelling is one of the best bits about parenting for me.

- **Crafty creations:** We're a very crafty family and we've always got a different project on the go. I've even learnt to embrace the mess that comes with it as part of the fun (though this did take a conscious effort and a shift in mindset to achieve!).
- **Tiny handhold:** Feeling my baby's hand in mine is a moment I try to enjoy every time it happens. The joy of that small, trusting grip is a heart-warming connection that I hope I will continue to cherish right through her childhood.
- **Bubble magic:** I keep bubbles in my handbag and any time that we need a bit of a pick-me-up, we blow bubbles and watch them float. Sometimes we chase them or pop them too. Always a giggle and such fun that makes me feel like a big kid.
- **Tickle fests:** My son loves to be tickled and I love hearing his laughter so I'm always looking for moments for little playful tickle sessions.
- **Noticing nature:** I try to look at the world through my twins' eyes, being curious about every little thing I see, smell or hear. Any time we step outside we're discovering bugs, leaves and all sorts of smells. It means building in extra time for every activity, but it's worth it because it brings a little dose of everyday joy to both me and the twins.
- **DIY masterpieces:** My teenage daughter and I like tackling DIY projects together. The joy of working on small home improvement tasks and the feeling of accomplishment is satisfying.
- **Music moments:** Dancing and singing in the living room is a bit of a thing in our family. The joy of moving to the rhythm and sharing music always feels fun.
- **Hugs and high-fives:** Offering comfort and celebrating achievements with hugs and high-fives offers little feel-good moments throughout our day.

- **LEGO® adventures:** We love building with LEGO and sometimes creating imaginative worlds. Other times we like to slavishly follow the instructions and make what's on the box. Either way, LEGO has always been a pretty constant source of joy for me and something that my kids now enjoy with me too.
- **Artistic showcases:** I like putting my kids' artwork on the fridge. Admiring their unique creations and feeling pride in their achievements is wonderful. It used to be finger painting and handprints, but over the years the fridge has come to look more like a bona fide gallery.
- **Puddle splashing:** Jumping in puddles after the rain. We love it. It just feels so good.
- **Grass picnics:** Picnicking on the grass in the garden or the park. Nothing fancy, just taking our usual lunch outside. It feels good and the moment I step outside I feel lighter.
- **Sandbox time:** Playing in our sandpit is something I especially enjoy with my son. I love the feel of the sand between my fingers and toes. It brings me real sensory joy and at the same time I feel like I'm doing good parenting as I'm throwing myself into playing with my son.
- **Starry nights:** Stargazing together on a clear night is something that often brings a little pocket of joy to my children and me. When I'm away, we find comfort in knowing we can all look at the same stars and it makes us feel a little closer.
- **Cartwheel celebrations:** My daughter celebrates every little victory with cartwheels. It started just as a way to burn off some of her boundless energy, but now it's just a little quirk of our daily lives and every time it makes me smile. I guess I smile at the absurdity of it, I smile at her pride and I smile at her joy and laughter which accompanies every turn.
- **Feel the love:** No matter how difficult the day has been, I like to look in on my children once they are fast asleep and look

angelic and just allow myself to connect with the deep love I feel for them. It can feel like a do-over after an especially tricky day.

Some people also shared the ways in which they found moments of joy in less family-oriented activities. These moments are important too as they can give us a minute to reset or take respite from the busyness of day-to-day parenting, which can help to prevent us feeling overwhelmed.

- **Play with pets:** My dog is my best friend. Playing fetch or simply cuddling with my furry companion fills my heart with joy. The unconditional love and connection we share is priceless.
- **Gardening:** My garden is my sanctuary. Planting flowers, tending to vegetables and watching them grow is a source of great joy. The sight of blooming flowers and the scent of earth keep me grounded and happy.
- **Self-care rituals:** Every evening, I indulge in a soothing bath. I use fragrant oils, light scented candles and just unwind. It's my way of self-love and finding joy in self-care.
- **Reading:** I read science fiction novels voraciously. Exploring different worlds and stories transports me, and I find immense pleasure in getting lost in a good book. I sneak in five minutes here and there in a busy day and can instantly be transported into another world.
- **Cooking:** Cooking is my creative outlet. Trying out new recipes or perfecting an old favourite brings me joy. Even if I'm cooking something for the hundredth time, I try to tap into the feeling of enjoying the process.
- **Collecting:** I started collecting action figures years ago. I know the story of every one and take great joy in looking at them, organizing them and deciding which figure I should collect next.

- **Watching:** We live on a busy street and I love to just observe the world go by from an upstairs window. Making up stories and imagining the days of the people who pass by my house is a funny little habit I have that I indulge in most days, and it makes me smile. Some people I've been watching for years but never spoken to. I have a whole soap opera in my head that is informed by their pace, gait or choice of clothes that day, but I've no idea if the lives I've created for my 'friends' matches up to their reality, and it doesn't matter. It's just a moment of escape from the pressures of my own life.

- **Cold callers:** I love seeing how whacky a story I can tell to cold callers on the phone. I try and come up with the most outlandish responses I can to their scripted conversations and see how long it takes them to go off-piste. It's stupid, but it makes me smile and means I look forward to cold calls whereas they used to bring me out in a cold sweat.

- **Mindful observing:** I sit by the window every morning and watch the sunrise. Observing the world without judgement brings me a sense of connection to the universe.

- **The first cup of coffee:** The first cup of coffee of the day is a special moment for me every day. It never gets old. I always make sure to take a couple of minutes to revel in it.

These moments of respite and self-care are equally vital, offering a brief pause to reset and recharge. They remind us that taking moments for ourselves is not selfish: it's essential for maintaining our wellbeing as we navigate the demands of parenting.

So, whether you're celebrating the joys of a shared meal or escaping into the world of your favourite book, remember that parenting is not only a journey of growth and challenges but also a journey filled with countless moments of joy, both big and small. Try to embrace these moments, savour them, and let them illuminate your path as a neurodivergent parent, making each day an adventure.

YOUR TURN

Now it's time to pause for a moment and reflect on your parenting journey, exploring the unique moments of joy that have brightened your path.

Take a moment to reflect on your own journey as a parent and the joy you've discovered in everyday activities. How do you currently celebrate these small moments with your child? Are there specific experiences you've shared that stand out as particularly joyful?

....

....

....

....

Think about the activities you and your child enjoy together. How can you amplify the joy in these shared moments? Are there new, simple rituals you can create to further connect and bond with your child?

....

....

....

....

Consider the pace of your daily life. Is it filled with hurried routines, or do you allow for moments of spontaneity and presence with your child? Reflect on ways to slow down and fully immerse yourself in the joy of parenting.

....

....

....

....

Reflect on how you capture and document these everyday joys. Do you keep a journal, take photographs, or simply hold them close in your memory? Explore creative ways to preserve and cherish these moments for both yourself and your child.

....

....

....

....

Take a moment to think about the future. How can you continue to find and celebrate joy in everyday parenting as your child grows? Are there new activities or experiences you'd like to explore together?

....

....

....

....

Consider discussing these ideas with your child. How do they perceive these moments of joy in your daily life? What are their favourite shared activities?

....

....

....

....

Engaging in a conversation with your child about these topics can deepen your connection and understanding of each other.

CHAPTER 19

Quick Read: Celebrating Positives and Reframing Negatives

Sometimes parenting can feel like a game we're losing. Many of the parents and carers I spoke to had a sense of always having more they felt they should be doing and not feeling good enough in the role of parent or carer. However, when we stopped to take time to notice the little things that were going well and revel in the tiny triumphs of the everyday, there actually was a lot to celebrate.

This is something I personally worked really hard on when my girls were little, with the support of my therapist, who helped me to question and reframe many of my regular thoughts about parenting and look for evidence for an alternative point of view in the little things that I could observe in day-to-day life.

For instance, I used to worry about whether I was doing enough as a parent, especially during those moments when it felt overwhelming. However, with the guidance of my therapist, I began to realize that parenting isn't about being perfect but about being present. I started noticing how my children's faces would light up when I joined them in their activities, even if just for a short time. Whether it was building a fort out of blankets, having a tea party with their stuffed animals, or simply listening to their stories, these small moments of connection became my reminders that I was doing something right as a parent.

It can help, too, to imagine things from the perspective of others looking in, and imagining how they might judge you kindly rather than harshly. A real-life example of this for me was in the early days after Ellie had joined our family and was currently in foster care with us. Her social worker paid a surprise visit (this really was a surprise as we lived 300 miles from Ellie's previous home and her social worker). As I saw Thérèse stood at the door my heart was in my mouth. We were just finishing our lunch and were tucking into some very ripe peaches. The girls were both under one, and we were doing baby-led weaning where the babies would feed themselves on solids as they were ready rather than being spoon-fed purée. The mess was indescribable. There was peach all over the girls. All over the table. All over the floor. Lyra, Ellie, myself, Tom and my mother-in-law were all crammed around this tiny table. My first thought was 'Thérèse will think I'm failing and take Ellie away,' because of the chaos she was stepping into. She later told me that I couldn't have been more wrong, that the moments she had spent quietly watching my family messily enjoying our peaches before she'd rung the doorbell was the point at which she became more certain than she'd ever been that this was the right place for Ellie to be. So where I saw disaster, my social worker saw triumph – a family connecting, children enjoying food and a lot of joy and laughter. I return to this moment often and consider how I might find small triumphs in my day-to-day if I viewed it through the eyes of someone a little kinder and more compassionate than myself.

When I spoke to the community about the small triumphs they could celebrate and the negatives they could reframe, these were the ideas they shared.

- **A lived-in loved home:** I used to stress over having a perfectly clean house, thinking it was a measure of my competence as a parent. But as I shifted my perspective, I began to appreciate the fingerprints on the windows and the scattered toys on the floor as signs of a lived-in, loved home. I realized that these 'messes' were actually symbols of a house filled with laughter, creativity and joy.

- **Button triumphs:** I love celebrating my son's accomplishments, like buttoning his own clothes. It's a small victory but it was hard won so every single time he does it, it's a big source of pride and joy.

- **Homemade creations:** Instead of fretting over perfect Pinterest-worthy crafts, I started embracing the delightful imperfections in the art my children created. Those finger-painted masterpieces and lopsided clay sculptures became tangible tokens of their creativity and a source of pride.
- **Bedtime adventures:** Bedtime can be challenging, but I found joy in creating a bedtime routine filled with stories, cuddles and whispered dreams. Those moments of connection at the end of the day became opportunities for bonding and sweet goodnight memories. I try to focus now on the little moments that are good even if they've followed BIG bad moments.
- **Kitchen chaos:** Cooking with kids can be messy, but I learned to find joy in the process rather than just the end result. The flour fights, chocolate chip mishaps and giggles in the kitchen made for some of our most cherished family moments.
- **Delayed gratification:** Instead of focusing on immediate rewards, I started celebrating my child's ability to wait for something they wanted. It might be waiting their turn at the park or saving their pocket money for a special toy.
- **Homework hurdles:** Rather than getting frustrated over homework struggles, I began to appreciate the effort my child put into their studies. Each question they asked or concept they grasped became a small victory.
- **Mismatched outfits:** My kids love to pick their own clothes, and sometimes their outfit choices can be quite eclectic. I learned to see it as an expression of their individuality and creativity, celebrating their unique style (though I do always find myself telling people 'They dressed themselves!').
- **Chaos to cooperation:** Sibling rivalry and arguments used to stress me out. However, I reframed these moments as opportunities for my children to learn conflict resolution and cooperation. When they resolve their disputes independently,

it feels like a parenting win (it doesn't happen all the time, but when it does it feels good).

- **Loud laughter:** Instead of shushing my kids when they got too loud, I began to consciously cherish the sound of their infectious laughter. Their joyful noise became a reminder of the happiness they brought into our home.
- **Exploring curiosity:** I started celebrating my child's endless questions and curiosity about the world. Each 'why' and 'how' was a sign of their eagerness to learn and explore.
- **Spontaneous adventures:** Instead of sticking to rigid schedules, I embraced spontaneous outings and adventures with my children. Those unplanned trips to the park or impromptu picnics became memories of carefree fun. They don't always go right, but when they do they are some of the best days we ever have because we start with no expectations.
- **Messy outdoor play:** Outdoor play often means muddy clothes and dirty hands, but I started to view it as a chance for my children to connect with nature and explore the world around them rather than just an inconvenience.
- **Growth through mistakes:** I encouraged my children to see mistakes as opportunities to learn and grow. Each mishap or setback became a stepping stone towards resilience and success. I'm working on seeing my own mistakes this way too, which is a little harder.
- **Comfort in routine:** Whilst I used to see routine as monotonous, I learned to appreciate the stability and comfort it brought to my children's lives. Predictable routines offered a sense of security.
- **Tiny achievements:** I discovered the joy in celebrating the tiniest milestones my children achieved. Whether it was successfully spelling a tricky word or managing to stack a tower of blocks, these mini-victories became opportunities

for family cheer. We made it a tradition to capture these moments with a quick snapshot and shared them in our family WhatsApp group, spreading the happiness.

- **Spontaneous acts of kindness:** The unexpected hugs, kisses and acts of kindness from my children warmed my heart. I internally celebrate their loving gestures.
- **Teamwork:** When my children cooperate on a game, a project or a chore, I take a moment to notice and celebrate their ability to work together and support one another.
- **Laughter in learning:** I found joy in the moments when learning became fun and laughter-filled, for example, when my son and I were practising maths problems, and he came up with a silly, imaginative answer that made us both burst into laughter. These were the moments when education became more than just lessons.
- **Innocence and wonder:** I celebrate my children's innocence and wonder. Their ability to see the world with fresh eyes and boundless curiosity is a daily source of inspiration and I try to see the world through their eyes.

In the intricate tapestry of parenthood, we often find ourselves navigating a landscape filled with moments of doubt and self-criticism. The journey can seem overwhelming, and it's easy to question whether we're doing enough or doing it right. But amidst the challenges, there are countless small triumphs waiting to be celebrated, and there's a way to reframe the negatives into positive perspectives.

Just like a beautiful mosaic is formed by arranging countless tiny pieces, our role as parents is crafted from these small moments of connection, laughter and joy. It's not about striving for perfection; it's about being present in our children's lives and embracing the delightful imperfections that make our journey unique.

As we've explored, it can be a powerful shift to see the world through the eyes of kindness, both from others and towards ourselves. In the midst of chaos, we might discover triumph, and in moments of vulnerability, we can unearth strength. Celebrating the lived-in, loved home with its fingerprints on the windows, the unique style of our children's clothing choices, or even the joy of cooking together can transform our perspective.

The journey of parenthood is not just about teaching and guiding our children but also about learning from them. Their curiosity, their innocence and their boundless wonder offer us inspiration and fresh perspectives.

YOUR TURN

As we conclude this chapter, let's shift from understanding to action. The 'Your Turn' activities ahead provide a practical way to apply the insights you've gained. It's where theory meets your unique parenting journey.

Think about a moment when you've judged yourself harshly as a parent. Write down the details of that moment and how it made you feel. Then, consider how someone kind and understanding might have viewed that same situation.

....

....

....

....

Create a unique ritual for celebrating small triumphs with your child. It could be a simple clap, a secret handshake or a special dance. Teach your child this ritual, and use it every time you both celebrate a tiny victory. Share the details of this ritual and its significance.

....

....

....

....

Imagine viewing your parenting journey through the eyes of someone incredibly kind and compassionate. Write a letter to yourself from this perspective, highlighting all the positive aspects of your parenting. This exercise can be a powerful way to reframe your self-criticism.

....

....

....

....

List three small triumphs or positive moments from your recent parenting experiences. How did these moments make you feel, and how can you celebrate them?

1. ....
2. ....
3. ....

Write about one thing you're grateful for in your parenting journey today. It can be anything, for example, a tiny triumph, a moment of connection or a shift in perspective.

....

....

....

....

Remember, your journey as a parent is a unique tapestry woven from these small moments. Embracing the positives and reframing the negatives can transform your perspective and bring more joy into your life as a parent. Enjoy these activities and continue to celebrate the everyday triumphs along the way.

CHAPTER 20

Quick Read: Building Belonging through Shared Passions

We previously explored the respite and joy that special interests can bring us as neurodivergent adults and parents. Now we're going to build on that idea by exploring how our hobbies and interests can help us to find a sense of belonging and connection which can fuel our wellbeing and build our capacity to live and parent well.

I now can't imagine how I managed without my hobbies and interests to keep me well. Introducing this aspect to my life, which had previously been focused exclusively on work with a side helping of parenting, has been a really healthy addition for me. I'm now taking the next steps with my hobbies and interests and trying to form connections and a feeling of community through the things I love to do.

For example, in my bouldering, I have recently started training to become a route setter. This means my local climbing wall lets me loose with power tools and I'm trusted to put the routes on the wall and test them out, as well as simply climb them. Becoming accepted as part of the in-house team that does this work has been a real boost for me as it's helping me to get to know more members of the local climbing community in a way that feels manageable for me because I have a prescribed role and there is learning involved. It's also given me a great reason to engage with people at the climbing wall as I look for feedback on the routes I've set and I've also started to do this a little online too, sharing the thinking behind my routes on Instagram and TikTok and using this as a way of engaging with, and feeling part of, a wider climbing community.

I've also been taking steps with my paragliding to become an active member of the community. I've been invited to join our local club's committee as their first women's officer, promoting the role of women within the sport, where we are traditionally very underrepresented. This not only deepens my engagement with a hobby I'm passionate about, but also provides a meaningful purpose. Additionally, it offers a role where I feel comfortable connecting with my fellow paragliders and supporting new pilots.

These new roles both feel like quite big undertakings, though, and you don't always need to take on extra work or an official role to feel more connection. My first steps at my climbing wall were to challenge myself to start conversations with fellow climbers who were often at the wall, meaning that the anonymous people around me slowly started to become my climbing friends, giving me a sense of community. I've been even more motivated to do this since Ellie has been joining me in many of my sessions as I am keen for her too to feel a sense of community and joy in her climbing rather than it being a solo endeavour. To that end, we've also recently started a bouldering group for home-educated children to help Ellie find a community closer in age to herself, and helping to set this up has also enabled me to connect with other home educators.

I find building relationships hard, but I'm slowly finding that by creating ways in through the things I'm passionate about and enjoy doing, and which mean I can connect in places and about topics that feel safe and comfortable, I can build a community around me that contribute a lot to my everyday life. Even though these things take up time, they somehow seem to free up mental capacity for my role as a parent as I feel happier in myself, and the incidental conversations I can have working through the niggles of daily parenting life with my fellow pilots or climbers can be deeply reassuring and helpful too.

Finding belonging and connection through our hobbies, passions and interests can take quite a big dose of bravery, but it can also prove very worthwhile. When I asked the community to share their experiences in this regard, this is what they chose to share:

- **Painting my way to connection:** I found solace in painting, joining a local art group. Expressing my emotions through art not only brought me joy but also connected me with fellow artists who understood the challenges of parenting a neurodivergent child.
- **Theatre enthusiasts:** I joined a local theatre group, diving into the world of acting alongside others who share a passion for the stage. Being able to step into different characters has really helped me explore the complex range of feelings I experience as an AuDHD [a person with coexisting autism and attention-deficit hyperactivity disorder] adult and parent.
- **Cooking up friendship:** Cooking became a shared passion for our family. Hosting themed dinner nights with friends and other parents allowed us to bond over the joy of preparing and savouring delicious dishes. These culinary gatherings offered support and understanding, creating a network of like-minded individuals.
- **Beachcombing club:** Beachcombing became my serene escape, and I found a welcoming group of fellow beach-combers. Our shared interest in collecting seashells and beach treasures enriched our lives and provided a peaceful refuge for discussing our challenges.
- **Hiking for my heart:** My love for hiking led me to join a local hiking club. Exploring the great outdoors not only provided an escape from daily stressors but also introduced me to a welcoming community of fellow hikers who shared my passion. This connection made it easier to navigate the challenges of parenting and to get away from them for a while too!

- **Singing together:** Singing in a community choir became a joyful outlet for me and knowing a tonne of songs by heart has been helpful in those stressful moments at home, I just start singing and things start to feel a little bit better right away.
- **Reading my way to belonging:** My passion for reading inspired me to join a book club. Connecting with others who shared my love for literature deepened our connections and provided an opportunity for intellectual discussions which were so welcome as I felt my brain turned to mush when my babies were small.
- **Board games and bonding:** Board games became a bonding point for our family. We organized game nights with friends, creating an inclusive and enjoyable space for our child to connect with peers and develop essential social skills, which also gave me and my husband a great excuse to play all our favourite board games too.
- **Stargazing nights:** I found a stargazing group where I could connect with fellow cosmos buffs. I'd always been a bit shy about this geeky hobby but my growing respect for the others in the group has helped me feel confident pursuing my passion and encouraging my children to lean into the things they love too, even if those things aren't cool.
- **Nurturing with nature:** We love being outside, so my son and I joined a local voluntary group that helps to keep the woods on our doorstep clean and tidy. It's a bit of litter picking, a bit of weeding and chopping back, a bit of drinking flasks of hot chocolate in the rain and a lot of joy. It's nice because we often walk in those woods and we feel a sense of pride that we're contributing to making them feel like such a special place.
- **Cycling to connect:** Inspired by my love of cycling, cycling became a shared passion for our family. We've been lucky

enough to find a supportive local network of cyclists. This not only brings us joy but also allows our children to participate in an activity that promotes physical health and social interaction.

- **Capturing life through a lens:** My passion for photography led to me meeting a range of other photographically minded parents online through a social platform which encouraged photo journaling. We'd share a photo each day and write a little about it. There were all sorts of different people using the site, but I connected most with other parents. This started years ago and many of them have become lifelong friends who've continued to share their parenting journey with me, offering smiles and reassurance along the way.
- **Craft beer enthusiasts:** Bonding with other parents over craft beer became a delightful hobby. It started as an excuse to grab a beer and have a moan, but visiting local breweries and sharing new brew discoveries has really helped us build connections whilst taking a break from parenting.
- **Exploring local history:** A group of parents with a passion for local history organized historical walking tours. These tours not only allowed us to connect with each other but also offered an educational and engaging experience for our children, some of whom were home-educated.
- **Nature sketching:** Having not picked up my pencils since school, I recently rediscovered the joy of nature sketching and joined a local group of artists. I really lose myself and it's been lovely to sketch just for fun. I'm not great at it, and that doesn't matter. It feels like good role-modelling for my son as I'm stepping outside my comfort zone and doing something just because it feels good and I like the people.
- **Finding peace through yoga:** A love for yoga led to the formation of a neighbourhood yoga class – we set up our own as we really wanted our children to be able to attend

> alongside us and for the costs to feel manageable. Practising yoga together not only enhanced the wellbeing of parents but also introduced our children to mindfulness and relaxation techniques.

In our exploration of connecting through shared passions, we've uncovered a profound truth: our interests and hobbies, which have long provided solace and joy, possess the remarkable ability to forge meaningful connections with others who share our enthusiasms. These connections offer us a sense of belonging and understanding that, in turn, enriches our wellbeing and empowers us in our roles as parents of neurodivergent children.

The stories and experiences shared by our community stand as a testament to the potential of these connections, providing strength, understanding and moments of respite in our journey of neurodivergent parenting.

YOUR TURN

As we transition to the 'Your Turn' section, I invite you to reflect on your own interests and hobbies, and how they can serve as gateways to meaningful connections.

Consider the hobbies and interests you've explored throughout your life. Have any of these pursuits provided you with a sense of belonging or connection with others, even in small ways? Reflect on these moments.

....

....

....

....

Have you ever considered joining a group or community related to one of your passions? Whether it's a local club or an online forum, think about how such a community could enhance your life.

....

....

....

....

If you're not already part of a community related to your passion, what's holding you back? Are there fears or barriers preventing you from taking the first step? Write about these and consider how you might overcome them.

....

....

....

....

Reflect on the people you've met through your interests, even if these connections weren't immediately obvious. Have you ever struck up conversations with like-minded individuals, even in passing? How did these interactions make you feel?

....

....

....

....

Are there interests or hobbies you've always wanted to explore but haven't had the chance? How might these new endeavours introduce you to a community that aligns with your passions?

....

....

....

....

Think about the challenges you face in building relationships. How might your interests serve as bridges to connect with others who understand your journey?

....

....

....

....

Consider small steps you can take, like starting conversations or reaching out to like-minded individuals, to gradually build a sense of community.

....

....

....

....

Revisit the stories shared in this chapter about individuals finding connections through their passions. Which of these resonates with you the most, and why?

....

....

....

....

Based on your reflections, set one or two goals for yourself to take steps towards connecting through your passions. Make them specific and achievable.

....

....

....

....

CHAPTER 21

Quick Read: Moments of Joy

As we draw to the end of this book, I wanted to end on a positive note, so I asked the community whose ideas populated this book to share their moments of joy as neurodivergent parents and carers. I hope they make you smile and spark a little joy and hope as you move forward in your parenting journey.

> 'When we enter the world of parenting, despite the painstaking slog it can sometimes be, we enter a world more delicious than Wonka's factory, more magical than Hogwarts and more fantastical than the Matrix. We become part of a journey where possibilities are created on new planes that would otherwise have been obscured from the grey, grey world of averages.'

> 'There are many moments within our household that bring me joy, but my absolute favourite is when we're all in the same room but doing our own special interests separately. Everyone is relaxed, feels comfortable, and yet we're spending time as a family. Sometimes I look around and see this and it makes me very proud and happy with my altogether different kind of family.'

> 'Mine is probably when I got a merit on my PGCert and PGDip autism studies with Sheffield Hallam University at the age of 42! I barely passed any GCSEs due to personal and learning needs.'

> 'Although I don't have children of my own, I have known my step-daughter since she was three and she is now 15. I never wanted to be a parent, and, although there have always been times when I've struggled greatly, I'm very proud of the relationship we have formed. I anticipated teenage years to be the hardest, but (touch wood and so far) they've been brilliant. I was unsure about "coming out" as autistic to her, but she has been the very best person to tell.

It's brought us closer, and I feel a sense of respect, tolerance and understanding from her like nothing I've experienced from anyone else I've spoken with about my autism.'

'A moment of parenting joy was when my son passed his GCSEs and went to New York with the school. He'd spent most of his early years in hospital, and was completely non-verbal and in a specialist nursery until the age of five.'

'After years of trying to influence the school I worked in to be autism aware and friendly, which was a lot like banging my head against a very hard brick wall, I was employed by a national charity as an autism adviser. I am finally listened to and am making a positive difference in schools in my area. That brings me joy on a daily basis.'

'The other day my daughter turned around and said, "I love you Mum," and I said, "Even though I'm not like other mums?" and she said, "BECAUSE you're not like other mums".'

'The day me and my son went to our first comic-con we walked into a different world. It was a world that felt so much better and easier than the one we'd just left behind. We spent all day with these massive grins on our faces. It was the best day ever.'

'Watching my children unmask and learn to accept themselves brings me great joy.'

'I've found joy through finding peace within myself and accepting myself and knowing that life is hard for me at times so it's okay to just stop, rest and look after myself.'

'My moment of joy is seeing my autistic daughter graduate from the University of East Anglia in the subject she loves. Knowing that this absolutely plays to the strengths that she has ALWAYS had.'

'Like me, my daughter has an incredible sense of smell. We'll be walking down the street and one of us will notice the scent of roses. We'll scan the environment and work out where the smell is coming from, then we'll go there together and breathe it right in. That smell brings us both such joy, and makes us each think of the other when we're apart too.'

'It is so hard to single out one specific moment of joy as a neurodivergent parent, because truly every day with my daughter is a blessing and she is the absolute joy of my heart. She's almost an adult now, but every age has been special in its way. I've enjoyed all the little achievements, the pleasure she gets from small things, the things she has taught me about looking at life, and also the things she has taught me about myself. I love to hear her opinions, her dreams for the future, and when she says she is pleased with herself. The journey from baby to 18-year-old has not all been easy. There have been difficult times and things I'd like to have done differently, but I am so proud of her and the person she is. I guess, then, that the day she was born – that is my moment of joy.'

'Dancing barefoot in big summer rain with my children. Playing, laughing and not giving a hoot what onlookers might think, caring only about the joy of my children and the love in my heart.'

'Writing stories with my son. We both have a million ideas a minute so you never know where the story will go, but you can be sure it will be fun.'

'Looking at my daughter who is taller than me now, and remembering the uncertainty I felt when I first held her in my arms. Would I be a good enough mother? I must have been, because now she is brilliant.'

Index